# Embroidery
## 200 Questions Answered

**Expert advice on everything from basic stitches
to finishing touches**

## Deena Beverley

For Nanny Rene, with love and gratitude for every precious moment

Search Press

A Quantum Book

Published in 2011 by Search Press Ltd.
Wellwood, North Farm Road,
Tunbridge Wells,
Kent TN2 3DR

This book is produced by
Quantum Publishing
6 Blundell Street
London
N7 9BH

ISBN 978-1-84448-660-1

All images are the copyright of Quantum Publishing. Many thanks to the following,
for providing worked examples:
Deena Beverley;  all examples apart from the following; Pat Cutforth;  36, 74, 121, 122,
181, Kath Danswan;  pages 11, 42, 77, 97, 108, 110, 113, 130, 153, 163, 184, Margaret
Gardiner; (from the author's collection), pages 161, 174, 189 Daisy Newton;  page 91,
Kira Wither-Jones; pages 48, 50a, 54, 55, 58, 59, 62, 63, 64, 66, 71, 72, 78, 80, 84, 85, 87,
88, 98, 99, 101, 102, 103, 106

# CONTENTS

# INTRODUCTION

Although freeform embroidery is often thought of as a very contemporary textile art, it has actually existed as long as the art of embroidery itself. The 11th century Bayeux Tapestry, for example, is not a tapestry at all, but an epic piece of freeform embroidery in wool on linen, featuring couched work and stem stitch.

Naturally, conventional techniques have their place, but gone are the days when stitching row upon row of perfectly symmetrical crosses counted out into neat repeating patterns was all that was meant by 'learning embroidery'.

After my first, fraught run-ins with a counted cross-stitch apron pocket I never quite came to grips with, the world of creative embroidery began to open up to me with the arrival of transfer kits.

Not to be disparaged as being a 'paint by numbers' textile art form, these kits actually offer embroiderers immense freedom to experiment with colour combinations, different yarns and stitch types. They are a great way to really familiarise yourself with new stitches and try out new techniques. The work of designing and transferring an outline on to the cloth has been done, leaving you to enjoy playing with colour, pattern and texture, embellishing the surface of the cloth in any way you like.

I have long been enchanted by the ability of a simple strand of thread to transform a piece of plain cloth. To me, a haberdashery counter is a calorie-free sweet shop full of irresistible treats. Beads and sequins are affordable jewels that add glamour to the subtlest stitching.

Following the basic instructions on that first kit, I learned how to work shaded satin stitch, French knots, stem stitch, and more. As the design took shape, satiny cotton threads gleaming against the darkness of the black cloth on which a simple white floral outline was printed, an alchemy of form, colour, and texture came into being which inspired me then and has continued to inspire me ever since. I spent my pocket money on stranded cottons and eagerly devoured every school library book on embroidery I could find.

At art college, a visiting tutor opened my eyes to the wider possibilities of embroidery as a truly freeform mode of artistic expression. Layering fabrics, reverse appliqué, stitches worked randomly without even a drawn pattern, let alone a transferred one, all became part of my repertoire. I discovered ways of incorporating all my treasured items into my work, in the form of adding found objects by freeform needlelace and couching down the ribbon and lace lengths I could not resist buying.

As my passion for including found objects in my work and a love of dolls-houses and miniatures almost equalled my enthusiasm for embroidery, it was inevitable that I found myself drawn to stumpwork, also known as raised embroidery. This most sculptural type of freeform embroidery is literally three dimensional. Reaching its peak of popularity in the seventeenth century, most early and, indeed, contemporary stumpwork is diminutively scaled.

However, one of the most thrilling aspects of freeform embroidery is its power to play with the rules as it sees fit, for whatever purpose is desired. A case in point is the Constance Howard-designed and group-worked piece 'The Country Wife', housed in the National Needlework Archive, UK. This staggeringly large scale (4.5m x 5m) mixed media freeform embroidered piece features three-dimensional figures that are almost life-sized, a world away from classical, miniscule stumpwork.

The power of embroidery to educate, entertain, enliven and enlighten has changed little since people first chose to stitch meaningful symbols on to their clothes, household goods and pieces for special occasions.

Embroidery has been around almost as long as clothes themselves. Earliest known examples date back to the Scythian horsemen of the 3rd and 5th centuries BC, who wore embroidered trousers, ending the idea that multiple freeform techniques are a new invention.

Oriental and Middle Eastern embroidery developed extensively and influenced European stitching, which was dominated by ecclesiastical depictions until the Renaissance.

Embroidery as a skilled professional craft eventually also became a popular pastime for those lucky enough to enjoy leisure time. A wide range of embroidery types evolved, and has continued to evolve ever since. Freeform embroidery is timeless. The earliest symbols used continue to inspire across cultural divides and the centuries today.

Happily, textile techniques are enjoying a renaissance of interest on the school curriculum. Happier still is the news that today's approach leaves the tyranny of counted cross-stitch as being the only embroidery skill taught far behind in the distant past. Between the pages of this book, I hope you will find the inspiration to set you on your own path of experimentation in embroidery, supported by straightforward practical help and some tips I have learned over the years. The journey is a colourful, diverse, and above all, enjoyable one. Happy Stitching!

# 1
# TOOLS AND MATERIALS

Just a few inexpensive tools and materials are all you need to start embroidering. Knowing how to choose and use the right tools and materials gives the best results and makes your stitching even more enjoyable.

# Question 1:
## What is freeform embroidery?

Freeform embroidery is the art of creating images, pictures and beautiful items using a variety of embroidery stitches, techniques and mediums. Freeform embroidery unlocks a world of experimentation and exploration.

This creative form of embroidery offers endless design possibilities using threads, yarns, fabrics, textiles, fibres, beads, ribbons, charms and found objects. Designs may be classic with a strong traditional focus or contemporary, original and abstract. Stitches may be controlled and even or worked randomly to create a variety of effects. Some freeform embroidery artists create 3D and sculptural images by working stitches over wire and other formers such as cardboard or metal.

*BELOW* A freeform embroidery piece worked by the author, featuring a hand-painted background, found objects, appliqué and hand-stitching.

# Question 2:
# How does it differ from cross-stitch?

Cross-stitch is a form of counted thread embroidery in which X-shaped stitches in an even-tiled pattern are worked to form a picture. Cross-stitch has a regular, highly recognisable, grid-like style, whereas freeform embroidery employs several different stitches to create a pattern. Freeform embroidery may be worked on a variety of fabrics. The image or pattern is hand-drawn or ironed on to the fabric using various transfer methods.

Cross-stitch is usually worked on an open and evenly woven fabric called 'aida'. This fabric allows the embroiderer to count the threads in each direction easily so that the stitches are of uniform size and appearance. This type of cross-stitch is also called 'counted' cross-stitch. Cross-stitch can also be embroidered on fabric that is purchased with a pattern of crosses printed on it. Once this printed material is stitched, a design emerges.

BELOW The expressive, freeflowing lines of freeform embroidery are a world away from the strict geometry of counted cross-stitch.

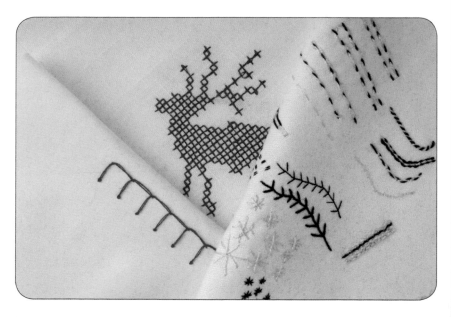

# Question 3:
## What is it used for?

The uses for freeform embroidery are endless. It can be used as an artistic form of decoration to embellish clothing, accessories, home décor or soft furnishings as well as creating unique freeform textiles and works of art.

# Question 4:
## What can I make or decorate with it?

You are only limited by your imagination! If you are new to embroidery, try your hand at embroidering a manageable-sized project or stitch sampler, as this success will encourage you to experiment further. Cushion covers, napkins, tablemats and tablecloths all lend themselves perfectly to this type of embroidery. Jazz up your clothing with some freeform embroidery on a blouse, skirt, pair of jeans or jacket. Friends will be delighted by practical and decorative gifts such as a glasses case, make-up bag or tote bag. Alternatively, you could simply frame your work and hang it on the wall.

*BELOW* Embroidering table linen is enduringly popular, adding colour to even the most everyday meals.

# Question 5:
# What type of stitches are used in this form of embroidery?

Any stitch may be incorporated into freeform embroidery. This style of embellishment actively encourages experimentation.

# Question 6:
# What equipment do I need?

The equipment required for freeform embroidery is essentially the same as for conventional embroidery. The basic requisites are needles, threads, fabrics, scissors, design transfer tools, hoops for stabilising the fabric while working and good lighting. Adventurous pieces can be created from even the simplest tools and materials. Imagination is the most vital requirement of all.

Optional materials are as diverse as the world around you. Beads, crystals, lace, ribbon, leather, wadding, shells, stones and assorted found items all have a place in freeform embroidery. Some of these may be more easily affixed to your fabric using specialised equipment – for example, jump rings and pliers make light work of attaching charms – but in most cases, simple tools and materials will suffice.

## EXPERT TIP
66 The sort of camping torch worn on, or integrated within a headband, gives great, shadowless lighting for stitching in the evenings. 99

# Question 7:
# What needles are used for freeform embroidery?

The type of needle you will need to use is dependent on the stitches, fabric threads and yarns you choose.

Crewel embroidery needles are fine needles with large, long eyes. The eye makes the needle easy to thread. Sizes 9-10 are used for fine embroidery. Larger sizes such as 3-8 are used for thicker, stranded threads and yarns.

### Chenille

This is a thick needle with a large eye, like a tapestry needle but with a sharp point. It is ideal for working with six strands of stranded cotton, metallic thread, ribbon or wool.

### Sharps

These are general-purpose needles ideal for fine embroidery. They are used for working with one or two strands of stranded cotton, silk or rayon. Sizes 10-12 are ideal for fine work, while sizes 7-9 are used for two to three strands of thread.

*LEFT TO RIGHT* Beading, Sharps, Embroidery/Crewel, Tapestry, Chenille.

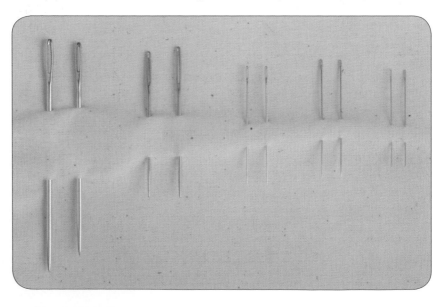

### Straw/Milliner's

A straw needle has a tiny eye no wider than the shaft of the needle. It is used for beading and for creating perfect wraps for French and bullion knots. Sizes 1-4 may be used for four to six strands of stranded cotton or yarns. The finer-sized needles, 5-8 and 9-11, are employed for finer work.

### Tapestry

This medium-length needle has a thick shaft and a blunt tip. It will separate the weave of the fabric rather than split the fibres and is used for decorative hem stitches, petit point and counted cross-stitch. The needles with the large eyes are used for working with wool and ribbons in freestyle embroidery.

## Question 8:
# How do I identify the correct size needle?

Needles come in a variety of sizes. The size of the needle is indicated by a number which is printed on the packaging that houses the needle — the higher the number, the finer the needle. Choosing the size of needle is sometimes confusing for a novice embroiderer. The eye of the needle should be of a similar size to the thickness of the thread or yarn that needs to pass through it so that the thread fills the hole left in the fabric by the needle.

*ABOVE* Choosing a needle appropriately sized to your thread means that your work will progress smoothly and with no unsightly holes or bunching.

# Question 9:
## What threads are commonly used?

A wide range of threads are used in freeform embroidery. Stranded cotton, silk, pearl cotton, wool, metallic threads, rayon, variegated threads, ribbons and various yarns are all suitably chosen for texture, scale and colour.

*BELOW* Threads are available in a mouth-watering array of colours and textures.

# Question 10:
## How do I stop the threads from knotting when I stitch?

Use short lengths of stranded cottons or threads so that the fibres don't become frayed from repeatedly being passed in and out of the fabric. If the thread begins to twist, hold the work upside down and let the needle hang freely. This will allow the thread to spin back to the correct amount of twist.

# Question 11:
# How do I store my threads?

You can store your threads in a chocolate box, a tin or even a shoe box. The most important consideration is to avoid excessive light or damp conditions. Store threads and yarns in a cool, dry place out of direct sunlight. There are many types of specialised storage systems available, and if you are planning to do a great deal of embroidery, it saves a lot of time to store your threads roughly grouped into colour families. Fishing tackle boxes and boxes for screws make excellent storage containers and often have transparent or translucent lids, making locating a particular thread quick and easy.

*BELOW* Tool boxes are perfect for organising threads into colour groups.

# Question 12:
## What type of fabrics should I use?

When you first start out, use inexpensive but stable fabrics like lightweight or openweave calico. Once you are confident with your stitch technique, you can expand to include a diverse range of fabrics, such as cotton lawn, silk, wool, furnishing fabrics, felt and linen.

*BELOW* Every fabric imaginable is useful to the creative freeform embroiderer.

# Question 13:
# How do I transfer a pattern on to fabric?

There are several methods used to transfer a pattern on to fabric. These include iron-on transfer paper, transfer pencils, direct tracing, templates, dressmakers' carbon, tacking, tulle and wash-away soluble fabrics.

One method popular with novice embroiderers is the use of iron-on transfers, manufactured with an image impregnated into a paper that, when pressed on to fabric using a warm iron, will leave a mark. These marks left on the fabric are permanent and must be embroidered over to be concealed. They are suitable for smooth-weave fabrics.

Even though this produces a design created by someone else, it is a quick and easy way to begin in embroidery, and by cutting the transfers up and rearranging them, you can begin to develop your design skills. Also, by experimenting with colour, texture and stitch, you will start to build a repertoire for use in original designs.

*BELOW* Iron-on transfers are a fun, easy way to start experimenting with freeform embroidery. Taking great care to hold the transfer in place at one point, make sure it has transferred fully before removing the iron.

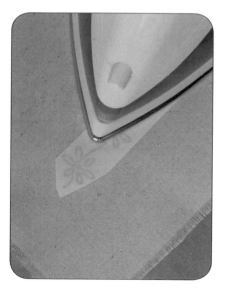

# Question 14:
## Where do I search for inspiration?

Inspiration is all around you. Keep an ongoing scrapbook filled with images clipped from magazines, as well as postcards and photographs. Carry a camera with you and take photos of flowers, insects and animals, gardens, landscapes and houses and any interesting textures that catch your eye. Camera phones are an invaluable tool for the freeform embroidery designer. Familiarise yourself with the macro setting so that you can take pictures of the sort of small-scale detail so inspiring to embroiderers.

*BELOW* Inspiration is everywhere – in the natural world, the objects around us and the materials we choose.

# Question 15:
## Which hoops would best suit my design?

Ideally, you will need to use a hoop that is large enough to encompass the whole design, allowing space around the image to avoid flattening the finished embroidery.

Frames may also be used, and there are several on the market that are ideal for working larger pieces. Some investigation into and experimentation with frames can be very worthwhile if you wish to further your interest in this form of embroidery. You may find, for example, that you work better sitting at a table using a hoop mounted in a stand, rather than in an easy chair with a handheld hoop.

*BELOW* Hoops are available in wood or plastic, handheld or tabletop.

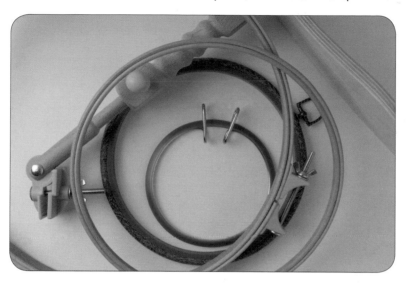

## Question 16:
# How do I store a piece when I can't finish it in one sitting?

Loosely wrap or cover the embroidery in a clean muslin or cotton cloth, and store in a cool, dry place out of direct sunlight or artificial heating. If your work is in a hoop and you know that you will not return to it for some time, remove it from the hoop so that the fabric is not unduly stressed or marked.

### EXPERT TIP
❝ Keep a screwdriver in your sewing box for tightening your embroidery hoop quickly and effortlessly. ❞

# 2
# HOW TO START

Since you will be starting and ending threads many times during a piece of freeform embroidery, it is worth learning the simplest, slickest ways of starting and finishing stitching, as well as transferring patterns and tensioning the ground fabric.

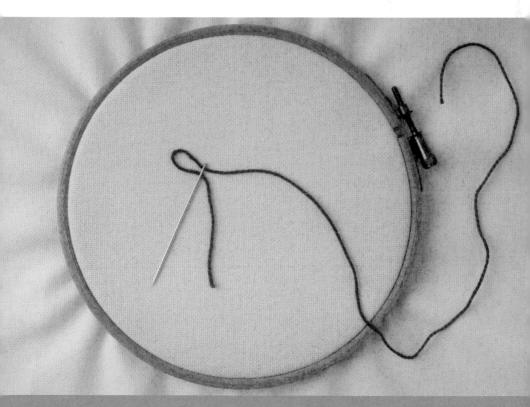

# Question 17:
## How do I thread a needle?

Select a needle of the correct size and type for the stitching you are to do. You need the eye of the needle to be large enough to take the thread smoothly through the fabric without force, but not so large that it leaves a hole around the thread as it passes through.

A number of proprietary needle threaders are available, and some stitchers find them invaluable. The most common type consists of a very fine, pointed wire loop approximately 2cm (¾in) long x 1cm (²⁄₅in) wide, attached to a small plastic handle. The wire loop is firm, yet pliable enough to pass easily through the eye of the needle. The thread is placed through this generously sized wire loop, and the loop is pulled back through the eye of the needle, bringing the thread with it. An alternative method, requiring no special equipment, is to loop the thread end tightly around the eye of the needle and then slip the loop off and push the folded thread through the needle's eye.

*BELOW* A needle threader is a handy device to aid the stitcher.

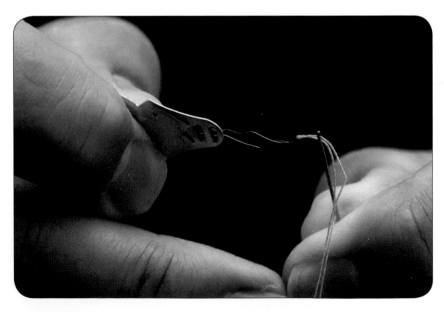

# Question 18:
# Why do I start work with only one strand of thread?

While you are developing confidence in embroidery, working with a single strand removes the frustration that can occur when working with multiple strands. It is all too easy to pull the different strands of stranded cottons through at different rates, resulting in tangling, although this settles down with practice.

*Coton perlé* (pearl cotton) is a very useful thread for those starting out in freeform embroidery. It has an attractive sheen, is twisted, which makes forming stitches simple, and is available in a variety of colours and weights.

Stranded cottons generally consist of six strands, which the stitcher divides into groups of two or three for working.

*RIGHT* Doubling back a thread makes it much easier to pass through the eye of a needle.

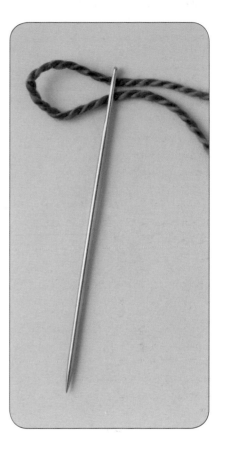

# Question 19:
## How do I tie a knot in my thread?

You don't! Or rather, do not be tempted to start stitching, leaving a knot behind your first stitch, as this will create lumpy work. To start stitching by the 'away waste knot' method, knot the end of your thread and insert the needle through the fabric, from the right side of the fabric to the reverse side, approximately 3cm (1¼in) from the position of your first stitch and along the line you are about to stitch.

Stitch towards the knot, enclosing the thread within the stitches at the rear of the work, before snipping off the waste knot and continuing to stitch as normal.

*TOP* An away waste knot, on the front of the piece.
*BOTTOM* Working back towards the away waste knot, as it looks on the reverse of the piece.

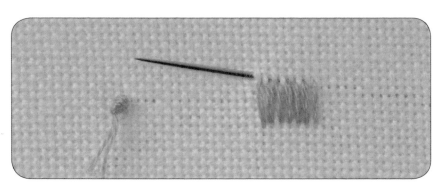

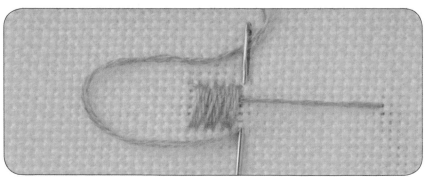

# Question 20:
# How do I fasten my thread to the back of my work when I finish stitching?

Take the needle and thread through to the reverse side of the piece. Work the thread through the back of the stitches for approximately 5cm (2in), taking care not to disrupt the stitches you are weaving through. Trim off the excess thread.

*BELOW* Fastening your work by running through your stitching on the back of your piece means that you don't need to make bulky knots.

# Question 21:
# What is thread tension?

Thread tension is a term referring to how tightly a stitch is made, or how tightly the thread is held during the construction of a stitch.

A piece of evenly stitched work demonstrates that tension has been well handled throughout. The more you stitch, the more familiar you will become with not only how to handle and vary thread tension, but what your natural inclination is. Some stitchers tend towards the very tight, while others have a looser touch. Neither extreme is, in itself, an issue, but if you know your own tensioning habits, you have a greater chance of working stitches accurately by taking care to compensate accordingly. For example, satin stitch needs a relaxed, but even, tension. If you know you tend towards tighter stitch formation, you can consciously ease off a little to achieve perfectly tensioned, smooth results.

# Question 22:
# Why is tension important when embroidering?

Learning how to tension thread appropriate to the stitch being made is a fundamental skill of embroidery. For example, when making a French knot, thread needs to be tensioned correctly when it is wrapped around the needle so that it forms an attractive knot. If the tension is too loose, a sloppy muddle of thread will be formed rather than a neat, controlled knot. Conversely, if the tension is too tight, a small, puckered stitch will result, with barely a knot visible on the surface at all, just an unappealing lumpiness in the fabric.

## EXPERT TIP

66 **Embroidery hoops are the simplest way of ensuring that you have even tension throughout your work.** 99

# Question 23:
# What are guidelines?

Although freeform embroidery is generally worked quite spontaneously, some stitches benefit greatly if some visual guides to their placement are established prior to working. These can be as simple as two faintly marked parallel lines denoting the width of a feathered chain stitch used as a border, for example, or a small sketched circle drawn as a guide for working a neat and even star stitch.

*BELOW* Guidelines make accuracy much easier to achieve when you are stitching regular patterns.

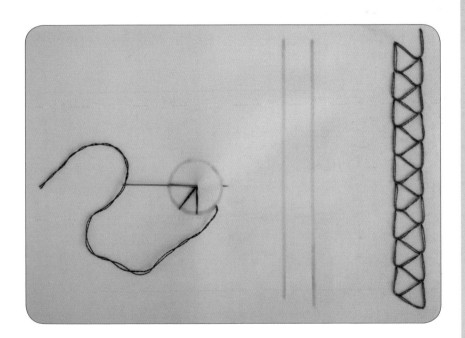

# Question 24:
# How do I transfer an iron-on design on to fabric?

Place a piece of aluminium foil on to a board with the reflective side facing up. Place the fabric right-side up over the aluminium foil. Pin the transfer face down on to the fabric. Press an iron firmly but carefully on to the transfer, taking care not to move the paper. It is important to read the manufacturer's instructions and not to scorch the material or blur the image.

## EXPERT TIP

66 Iron-on transfers have come a long way in recent years. Designs based on everything from vintage pin-up girls to rock-and-roll imagery are now available. 99

# Question 25:
# What is dressmaker's carbon paper?

Dressmaker's carbon paper is a useful, non-smudging product for transferring your own designs on to fabric, available from haberdashery and fabric shops. It is available in a range of colours; for best visibility, choose one which contrasts well with the shade of your ground fabric. Follow the manufacturer's instructions for best results. Ensure that your stitches cover the carbon lines so that they are not visible on your finished piece.

## EXPERT TIP

66 Experiment with the colour of carbon paper you are planning to use on an offcut of your fabric before transferring your whole design. 99

# Question 26:
# What is a light box?

A light box is a very useful tool for tracing out and developing designs. It consists of a sheet of translucent glass or plastic held in a box frame, generally tilted slightly, like an easel. This box houses lights that clearly illuminate a design taped in place on the glass or plastic screen. The design may then easily be traced off, ready for transferring to fabric.

*BELOW* It is worth investing in a light box if you intend on designing several pieces, as they make light work of transferring your pattern.

# Question 27:
## What is tacking?

Tacking, also known as basting, is a term to describe sewing with a long running stitch to mark out a piece of fabric, or temporarily secure paper to fabric or layers of fabric together.

Traditionally, tacking is a phrase used to describe this stitch when used to secure two or more layers, while basting refers to the stitch being taken through a single thickness of fabric. However, over time the terms basting and tacking have come to mean the same thing: temporary marking or fixing using a large running stitch, which can be worked quickly and removed easily when the piece is complete.

*BELOW* Tacking is essential for accuracy in preparatory work.

# Question 28:
# How do I transfer an image using tacking stitch?

The tacking stitch method works well on most materials, making it a good choice when dressmaker's carbon is not suitable, e.g. on very textured fabrics.

Trace your design on to tracing paper. Draw lines vertically and horizontally through the centre of the design. Press your background fabric flat and work a vertical and horizontal line of tacking stitches through its centre. Place your tracing on the right side of the fabric, ensuring that the centre lines meet,

and pin to secure. Using a colour thread that will show up clearly on your fabric, work running stitches along the pattern lines. Secure the beginnings and endings of each stitch line with a few backstitches. When you have finished tracing, gently tear away the tracing paper to reveal the transferred design. As you embroider, remove the tacking stitches.

*BELOW* Tacking through tracing paper to transfer a pattern works well on even the most textured and patterned cloth.

# Question 29:
# How do I transfer a pattern using water-soluble stabiliser?

You can trace your design on to water-soluble stabiliser, or print from a computer directly on to this useful medium, which is available in a variety of thicknesses from super-lightweight, transparent film to a sturdy, almost opaque, cotton-like mesh. Having transferred your design on to the water-soluble medium of your choice, simply tack the stabiliser to the right side of your fabric and work your embroidery through it. Some stitchers find that a substantial stabiliser stiffens and supports the ground fabric enough to enable embroidering without a hoop or frame. When you have finished stitching, carefully wash away the stabiliser following the manufacturer's instructions until all traces of it have been removed. The exception to this is if you wish to leave a small amount of the product within the fibres of your work to act as a stiffener – for example, if you are shaping your now dampened work around a form, such as an upturned bowl, so that it becomes a sculptural object, rather than a two-dimensional piece. If you want to try this, cover the form in cling film first so that it is easy to remove the bowl when the work has thoroughly dried.

*BELOW* Tracing a design on to water-soluble stabiliser.

*BELOW* Tacking water-soluble stabiliser on to the fabric.

# Question 30:
# How and why do I stretch the fabric to be stitched?

Although some people prefer to embroider with the fabric loose in their hands, most embroiderers find it more restful to support the base fabric in a hoop or frame of some sort. This greatly helps the even tensioning of stitches. It is particularly useful when creating stitches such as French knots, when not needing to hold the ground fabric taut frees up your hands to hold the wrapped thread in place as you work the stitch. Always press your fabric carefully before use and take care to keep the fabric square to the warp and weft as you gently ease it taut within your frame or hoop.

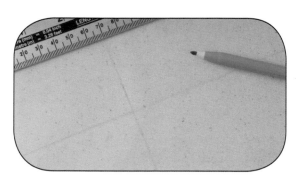

*ABOVE* Marking the warp and weft of the fabric prior to hooping up.

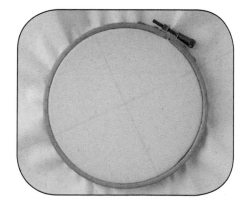

*RIGHT* Stretching the fabric on to the embroidery hoop.

# Question 31:
## What is bias binding?

Bias binding is a narrow strip of fabric that has been cut on the bias – a diagonal line taken at a 45-degree angle to the warp and weft of a fabric. Both its long edges are then ironed inwards. It is generally used to finish off a raw edge, and because the binding has been cut on the bias, it can stretch readily to accommodate curves, making it also ideally suited to being wrapped smoothly around a circular embroidery hoop.

*BELOW* Bias binding is available in a wide variety of colours and textures.

## EXPERT TIP
**❝ Cotton bias binding provides a better non-slip surface for binding a hoop than the satin variety. ❞**

# Question 32:
# How and why do I use bias binding on a hoop?

Wrapping your hoop in bias binding helps stop the fabric from slipping against the shiny wood or plastic of the hoop. Since the fabric is held under considerable tension in the hoop, binding helps reduce the likelihood of the hoop marking the fabric, and also helps prevent unwelcome wear and abrasion on the parts of the fabric in direct contact with the hoop. Bind the inner ring only with bias binding, wrapping it tightly around the hoop. Secure with a few small stitches.

*BELOW* Binding the inner ring of an embroidery hoop helps the fabric grip better and prevents the hoop from marking the cloth.

# Question 33:
# How do I hoop up and tension fabric?

## HOW IT'S DONE

**1** Separate the inner and outer hoops.

**2** Press your fabric. If using steam, allow fabric to dry and cool completely.

**3** Place the area to be embroidered over the inner hoop.

**4** Place the outer hoop over the fabric-covered inner hoop and tighten using the screw on the side of the outer hoop.

**5** Gently and evenly ease out the edges of the fabric so that the area to be embroidered becomes smooth and taut within the hoop. Take care to ensure that the warp and weft of the fabric remain true and square.

If you are working a large piece and need to move the hoop over and across the work, cover the embroidery already worked with a piece of muslin before rehooping. The muslin will help protect the stitches held between the two hoops. Secure the outer ring and cut away the muslin within the area you now wish to stitch.

If you are stitching a very small or awkwardly shaped piece of fabric, stitch it to a larger piece of material and support this in a hoop (see picture below). Then, on the wrong side of the fabric, carefully cut away the supporting fabric from inside the shape you wish to embroider.

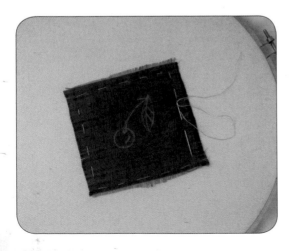

*LEFT* Tacking a small, precious piece of silk to a larger piece of inexpensive fabric makes it easy to hoop up and stitch. Simply cut away the calico from behind the silk before you start work.

# Question 34:
## What is a rotating hand frame?

Traditionally used in canvaswork, a rotating hand frame is a rectangular frame on which the fabric is stretched between rollers at the top and bottom. The frame must be wide enough to hold the entire width of the fabric, but the height is not important because as the work progresses the fabric can be rolled off one roller and on to the other to reach the required position.

Rotating hand frames are ideal for large projects. Generally, the top and bottom of the fabric is sewn on to two canvas strips attached to a pair of rollers. The rollers are clipped into the side bars, and the fabric is rolled up until it is tight. Some modern frames incorporate a clip system, or use tape and staples to hold the fabric, removing the need to stitch it to supporting strips.

# Question 35:
## What is a stretcher frame?

A stretcher frame is generally a wooden frame on to which a piece of embroidery is secured. It is possible to both work and mount your piece on the same stretcher frame. Clearly, this removes the need for restretching and mounting your work after stitching, making stretcher frames an attractive proposition for the busy embroiderer, despite the fact that they then cannot be reused for other projects.

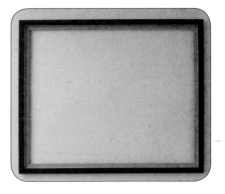

*ABOVE* Old picture frames make perfect stretcher frames.

# Question 36:
# How do I prepare a stretcher frame?

Choose stretcher bars appropriate to the size of your fabric. If you are planning to display your embroidery permanently on this stretcher frame, you may like to use decorative upholstery tacks for this job and conceal any raw edges of the fabric at the rear of the frame, secured with staples or drawing pins.

## HOW IT'S DONE

**1** Slot together the four interlocking sides of the stretcher frame and tap firmly into place with a rubber mallet or similar heavy implement. Place the frame on a flat surface.

**2** Take your pressed fabric and secure it to the frame using tacks. Start at the centre of the top and bottom of the frame and gently but firmly pull the fabric until it is taut.

**3** Follow this by tacking the centre of the left-hand, then right-hand side of the frame. Take care to ensure that the grain of the fabric remains square and true.

**4** Gently pull the fabric out towards the corners of the frame and secure each corner. Then add further securing tacks evenly along the gaps, easing the fabric to keep it taut as you work around the frame until it is entirely secure.

**5** Keep working on opposite sides – if you add a tack to the left, add one to the right; if you tack the top, tack the bottom.

**6** Be prepared that as the fabric becomes stretched it may give slightly, so you will need to reposition the tacks as you work. Finally lightly tap the tacks in place to secure the position.

# Question 37:
# What is a clip frame?

Adjustable wooden or plastic stretcher frames that are available clip together to form squares and rectangles. Experienced embroiderers often graduate to these after starting with embroidery hoops because these frames are simple and quick to set up, are kinder to the fabric, cause fewer marks, and allow for a larger working area than a hoop. The advantage of these frames is that they can be reused for other projects. The disadvantage is that they are not suitable for displaying your finished piece.

*BELOW* Clip frames are simple and quick to use, perfect for larger pieces of work where you need to move the frame several times during stitching.

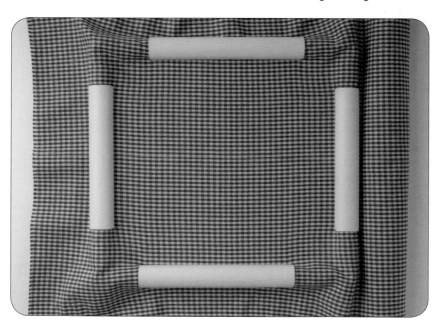

# Question 38:
## How do I use a clip frame?

Choose a frame to suit the size of your fabric. Simply clip the fabric to the bars and use the locking levers to secure the bars in place. Some of these frames can be made smaller or larger by moving the corner pegs into holes in the sides of the frame. Manufacturer's directions may vary slightly, so be sure to read carefully.

# Question 39:
## Why do I need to stitch a sample first?

Although it is not essential to stitch a sample, it is useful to have a spare piece of fabric stretched on to a hoop so that you can experiment with stitches, especially those unfamiliar to you. You may also like to try modifying a familiar stitch by altering its scale, which can dramatically alter its appearance, before committing your idea to your main piece of work.

Having a sample piece to work on is like having a sketchbook – you can play around with colour and texture combinations, perfect new stitch techniques and brush up on those you haven't used in a while. It helps take the pressure off the main piece you are working on and keeps stitching fun!

*ABOVE* Working a stitched sample allows you to experiment with new techniques and materials.

# Question 40:
# Where do I start stitching on a pattern?

Some designs will have an obvious place where stitching must begin. For example, if you are appliquéing shapes to your background, these will need securing in place before you can add any decorative stitching. If there are any areas which really define a piece, or which you are particularly concerned about, such as eyes on a face, you may feel happier embroidering these first. This both removes any feeling of pressure hanging over you, and means that if you are not happy with your work, you can simply unpick it and start again relatively easily, rather than tackle a densely stitched area. Otherwise, it is generally easier to stitch from the centre of a piece, working outwards, so that you are not in contact with stitched areas as you work. On a very large piece, such as one mounted on a rotating frame, you may choose to work from the top of the piece towards the bottom, rolling up the work as you go, but the joy of freeform embroidery is that truthfully, you can stitch where the fancy takes you.

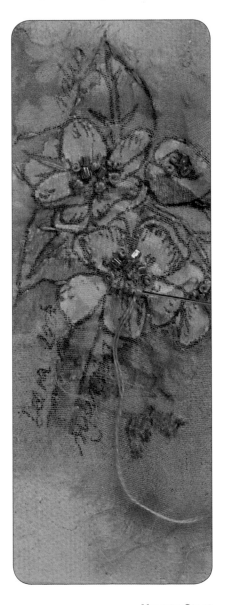

*RIGHT* French knots worked to secure the centre of an appliquéd piece handpainted by the author.

# Question 41:
## In what direction do I stitch?

Some stitches may be worked in any direction. This particularly applies to individual stitches such as bullion knots, star stitch and straight stitch. You can work such stitches randomly, or control the direction to produce a sense of movement. For example, a large number of straight stitches could be worked in a sinuous, waving pattern on a freeform embroidered portrait to suggest the movement of flowing hair.

# Question 42:
## Why are some stitches worked in different directions?

Some stitches are worked in specific directions for the simple reason that they are much more comfortable to work when stitched in the direction given. If you are left-handed, you may well find that you will want to reverse the direction, working the running stitch from left to right rather than the usually specified right to left.

### EXPERT TIP
**66 Think of stitches as brush strokes. Apply them with this in mind, and your work will look fluid and alive. 99**

# 3

# SIMPLE STITCHES

The basic embroidery stitches are the foundation of all the exciting stitches and techniques ahead of you. Alternatively, some noted embroiderers restrict themselves solely to these simple stitches, yet still achieve astonishingly diverse results.

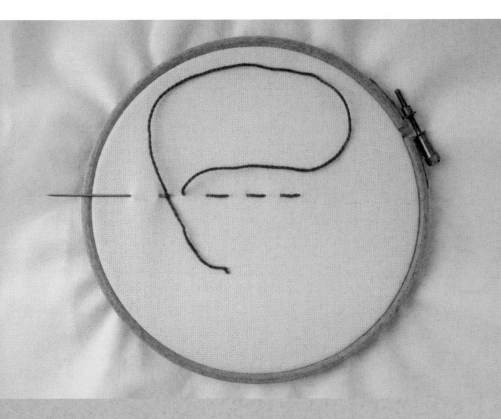

# Question 43:
## What is running stitch?

Running stitch, or straight stitch, is the basic stitch in hand-sewing and embroidery, on which all other forms of sewing are based. The stitch is worked by passing the needle in and out of the fabric, creating a broken line. Running stitches can be worked in varying lengths, but generally all the stitches on the right side of the fabric are of the same length. Running stitches are used in hand-sewing, dressmaking, patchwork and quilting.

This stitch is also a foundation stitch for other stitches, such as for example, padded satin stitch.

*BELOW* Rows of running stitch in three different sizes.

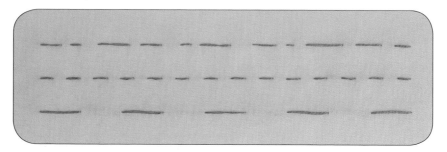

# Question 44:
## How do I work running stitch?

To work a running stitch, bring the needle up through the fabric, from the wrong side to the right at Point A, and then down through the fabric at Point B. Bring the needle up again at Point C, ensuring that the space between each point is consistent.

Continue. The length of stitches can be increased or decreased depending on the desired effect (see picture above). The length of each stitch and the spaces between can also be varied for an irregular look.

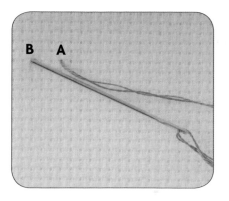

*ABOVE* Insert the needle back down through the fabric to make the first running stitch.

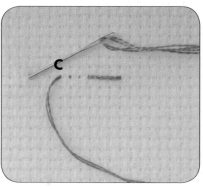

*ABOVE* Bring the needle back out through the fabric before reinserting it to make a line of running stitch.

# Question 45:
# What is stem stitch?

Stem stitch is an excellent stitch for following and defining shapes, and forms a useful foundation for more complicated stitches. Each stitch overlaps the previous stitch very closely to one side, forming a twisted line of stitching with the thread passing below the needle. It is generally used for outlining and for stitching flower stems and tendrils. The width and length of each stitch depends on the angle at which it is worked over the line. The thread can be kept either above or below the needle, but it must remain in that place at all times while you are stitching to ensure that the stitching looks the same.

*RIGHT* As its name suggests, stem stitch is perfect for depicting flower stems.

# Question 46:
## How and why is backstitch worked?

The stitches are made as the needle is passed through the fabric, working two stitch lengths forward, one stitch length back, along the line to be filled.

Backstitch, like stem stitch, is an outlining stitch. It is also used to stitch two layers of fabric together as it is a reinforced method of stitching.

Bring the needle up through the fabric from the wrong side to the right, at Point A. Reinsert the needle at Point B and emerge again at Point C. Insert the needle again at A, then go on an equal distance further on, past C. Continue in this way until the line is complete.

*BELOW* Backstitch is a strong and useful stitch to use.

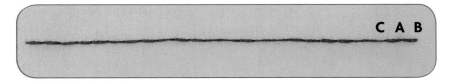

**C  A  B**

# Question 47:
## What is Pekinese stitch?

Pekinese stitch is a complex-looking stitch that is actually very simple to work, giving a rich, braided appearance for relatively little effort and expertise.

*BELOW* Pekinese stitch looks complex but is easy and fun to work.

# Question 48:
# How do I work Pekinese stitch?

Work a row of backstitches from left to right. Using a tapestry needle, bring a contrasting coloured thread up through the fabric from the wrong side to the right side at Point A. Take the needle up and through the second backstitch, then back down through the first backstitch without piercing the fabric. Keep the thread loop held beneath the needle as you continue to work along the line of stitches. You can pull the loops gently to ease them to a uniform tightness, or leave them looser for a different effect.

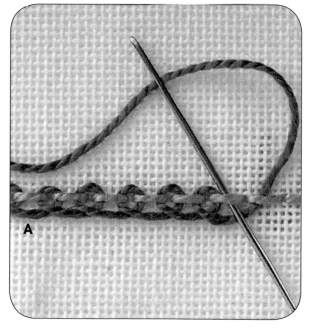

*RIGHT* Pekinese stitch comes from the group of stitches known as composite stitches, a combined stitch using two or more stitches to decorative effect.

**A**

# Question 49:
# What is couching, and why would I use it?

Couching means to secure a thread, ribbon or yarn to fabric using a different, usually finer thread. It is a technique used when the main thread, ribbon or yarn is too thick to pass through the ground fabric without causing damage.

Couching is probably one of the simplest, yet most exciting techniques available to the freeform embroiderer, since it offers an opportunity to secure a wide array of wild and wonderful materials and found objects to the surface of the fabric, without trying to pass them through the fabric itself.

Once you have started couching, you will find yourself looking at a much more diverse range of items as having potential for embroidery, where previously you might have restricted yourself primarily to conventional threads.

Twigs, leather, drinking straws, shells and sea tumbled glass are all suitable and interesting items for couching. Choose a thread or yarn for the couching stitch that complements or deliberately contrasts with the item you are couching, for example, using a rustic thread, such as a natural, textured thread to secure a knobbly twig.

*BELOW* Ribbon is just one of the many materials that can be couched in place.

# Question 50:
# How do I couch a thread, yarn or ribbon?

More regularly scaled threads and yarns can simply be brought up to the surface using any suitably sized needle, leaving the ends to the rear of the work and securing them there, unless a frayed-end look is required as part of your design. In couching down the laid thread, you can be as discreet and unobtrusive, or as bold and adventurous in your choice of thread colour, texture and scale as you like. Simply stitch across the length of the laid yarn, thread or ribbon sufficient to hold it in place according to your chosen design. Make your securing stitches small and neat or decorative and large. The decision is yours.

*BELOW* Couching is the perfect way to secure a thick rope to your ground fabric.

## HOW IT'S DONE

**1** Lay the thread, yarn or ribbon to be couched along the line to be stitched, making sure you cut enough to cover this length plus a little extra for starting and finishing off. If you are using a very wide material as your laid thread or 'rope' you will need to use the plunging method to start and finish your couched line, as follows.

**2** Leaving your sewing thread and small needle at the back of your work, make a hole in the fabric of sufficient size to accept the 'rope'. A stiletto is the perfect tool.

**3** Insert a large-eyed needle partially through the fabric, leaving the eye on the surface of the fabric.

**4** Carefully untwist the end of the rope so that you can feed each strand in turn through the large needle to be taken down through the fabric. Remove the large-eyed needle.

**5** On the reverse of the fabric, fold back and flatten out the rope ends and secure with small stitches wherever is most unobtrusive and convenient.

**6** Follow the outline of your design with the laid rope, securing with small, carefully tensioned stitches spaced so as to hold the outline in your desired shape. End your stitching with the same plunging method as you began.

*BELOW* Couched lines may be straight or curved. Here, the appliqué tulip has been edged with couching.

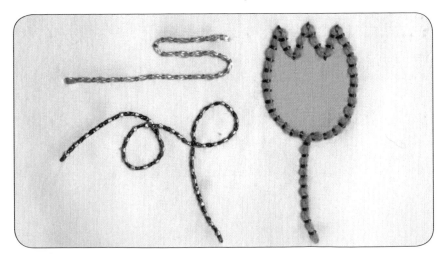

# Question 51:
# What is chain stitch?

This quick-to-work stitch can be used as detached stitches or in a line that curves easily, making this a highly versatile stitch.

Worked singly, chain stitch is often used to form leaves or flower petals. In this form it is also known as lazy daisy stitch, detached chain stitch or scattered chain stitch.

## EXPERT TIP

**❝ Chain stitches can be made wider by inserting the needle slightly to the right, instead of at the exact point where the last thread emerged. ❞**

*BELOW* Chain stitch is used here to connect diverse patchworked shapes.

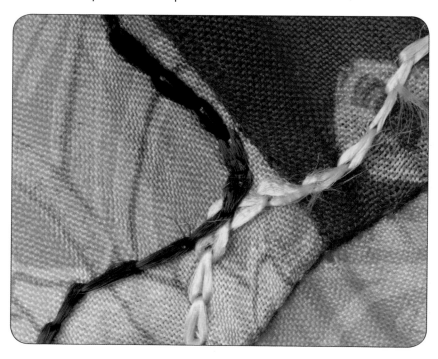

# Question 52:
# How and why do I work chain stitch?

Chain stitch is, after cross-stitch, probably the most universally known embroidery stitch. Now found worldwide, it appears to have originated from Persia and India. The earliest sewing machines produced chain stitch, and toy sewing machines still work chain stitch. Although generally worked as depicted here, chain stitch is also worked by the tambour hook or ari method, which speeds up the work.

In both methods, particularly used for working chain stitch on fine fabrics such as voile, the hook is pushed through the fabric and picks up the thread, bringing it to the top in a loop. The hook is taken back down through this loop before being brought up again with the thread, producing a chain stitch. In tambour work, a frame is used; in ari, the fabric is hand-tensioned only.

## HOW IT'S DONE

**1** Bring the needle through the fabric from the wrong side to the right side at Point A.

**2** Let the thread form a natural loop before reinserting the needle at Point A.

**3** Take care to leave the loop loose as you bring the needle up again at Point B, pulling through the working thread and leaving the loop sitting neatly on the surface. Make a small stitch over the loop to secure it in place, at the end of the chain.

*BELOW* Chain stitch worked in varying scales.

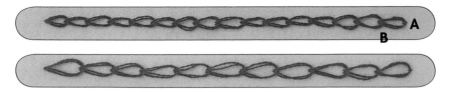

# Question 53:
# How and why do I work feather stitch?

Feather stitch is also known as single coral, or briar stitch. Although in itself a basic stitch, it is well worth mastering as it forms the core of a large group of looped stitches. It covers a lot of ground quickly and easily and is very fluid and flowing, lending itself to a diverse range of applications.

Feather stitches have long been used to decorate clothing, notably smocked items and in particular children's clothes. The stitches can be used to create outlines, fill shapes and work borders. Pictorially, as you'd expect from the name of the stitch, feather stitch can represent any featherlike form, such as areas of foliage, grasses, ferns and individual leaves or veining on leaves.

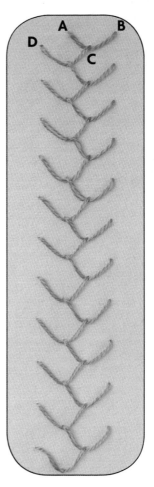

## HOW IT'S DONE

**1** Working from top to bottom, bring the needle up through the fabric from the wrong side to the right at Point A.

**2** Reinsert the needle at B, keeping a loop of thread beneath the needle.

**3** Bring the needle back up at C, leaving the distance between Points B and C the same as the distance between Points A and B.

**4** Pull the thread through and reinsert the needle at Point D, again making sure to hold a loop of thread beneath the needle. Continue making these alternating stitches.

*ABOVE* Feather stitch worked regularly.

**Simple Stitches**    57

# Question 54:
# How and why do I work herringbone stitch?

Herringbone stitch is also known as Russian cross-stitch, witch stitch, catch stitch, Russian stitch and mossoul stitch. A simply worked interlacing stitch, it is very useful for securing raw edges, particularly in non-fraying fabrics.

In shadow work – a type of embroidery worked on a sheer fabric where the stitches show through the fabric for a delicate, muted effect – herringbone stitch is worked with no space between the stitches to make two rows of backstitch on the reverse of the fabric. In this case, it is called double backstitch or closed herringbone stitch. This work often features on lingerie and infant's clothes, e.g. on christening garments.

## HOW IT'S DONE

**1** Working from left to right, bring the needle up through the fabric from the wrong side to the right at Point A.

**2** Reinsert the needle diagonally up and toward the right at Point B.

**3** Bring the needle back up again at Point C.

**4** Reinsert the needle diagonally down and toward the right at Point D. Continue until desired length.

*BELOW* Regular and irregularly worked herringbone stitch.

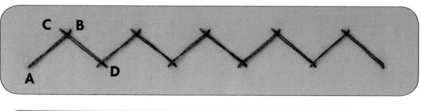

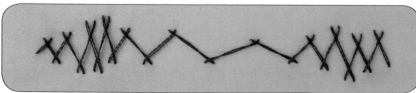

# 4

# MORE COMPLEX STITCHES

The stitches here build on all you have learned so far, and are not necessarily difficult to produce. For example, simply adding a thread whipped around a basic stitch creates a dramatic effect with minimal extra effort.

# Question 55:
# How do I work fly stitch?

Fly stitch is also known as the 'Y' stitch or the tied stitch. You can make the tail of this stitch as long as you like, as shown in the picture below. If you are working the stitch as a filling stitch, this makes a good, quickly worked filling — open, yet covering a lot of ground.

Adding fly stitches to each side of a double row of whipped chain stitches (see page 63, question 56 for how to work whipped chain stitch) produces a textural, attractive and wide border.

## HOW IT'S DONE

**1** Bring the needle up through the fabric from the wrong side towards the right at Point A.

**2** Reinsert the needle at Point B, taking care to leave a loop of thread on the surface of the fabric.

**3** Bring the needle up again at Point C, inside the thread loop.

**4** Reinsert the needle at Point D, securing the loop with a small stitch.

## EXPERT TIP

**66** A detached chain stitch worked in the 'v' of a fly stitch makes a quick, but effective, flower bud held in a calyx form. **99**

*BELOW* Fly stitch worked with and without a tail.

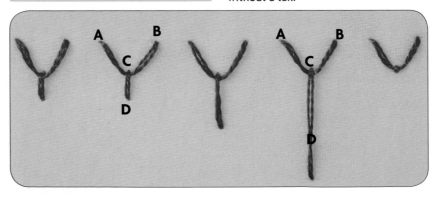

**More Complex Stitches**

# Question 56:
# What is whipped chain stitch?

Whipped chain stitch is simply regular chain stitch that has had a whipping stitch passed around it for a lively, textural effect.

Whipping stitches can be sewn in a contrasting or toning thread, depending on the effect you are aiming for. There are three ways of producing even a basic whipped chain, which gives you some idea of the versatility of this stitch. You can whip along one side of the chain stitch only, or along each side. Alternatively, take the whipping right around the entire chain.

A stunning, rich border can be simply made by working two rows of chain stitch next to each other before whipping them in a heavy thread in any of the three ways as described previously.

You could introduce extra interest and width to these neighbouring rows by adding fly stitches (see page 62, question 55 for how to work fly stitch) on each side.

*BELOW* Whipped chain stitch worked in straight and undulating lines.

## HOW IT'S DONE

**1** Sew a line of chain stitch. Using a tapestry needle, bring your whipping stitch up from the wrong side of the fabric to the right side, but just to one side of the first chain stitch.

**2** Pass the thread over and around the chain stitch only. Make sure not to go back down through the fabric.

**3** Thread the needle under the next stitch then pass it back over again.

**4** Continue until the last chain stitch has been whipped before reinserting the needle through the fabric.

# Question 57:
# What is shisha stitch and how do I work it?

The shisha technique of applying mica, coins or mirror glass to fabric using embroidery stitches was practiced particularly in areas of Pakistan and India before becoming popular in the Western world. Since the items being attached have no holes that may be stitched through to secure them to the cloth, they are held in place by a criss-crossed pattern of stitches.

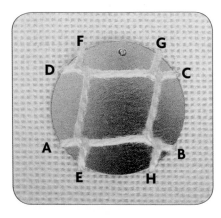

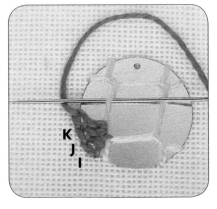

*RIGHT* Shisha stitch affixes mirrors to the fabric (see pictures on previous page) despite them having no securing hole.

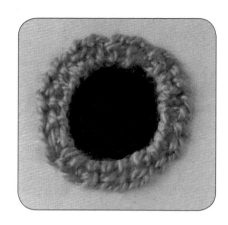

## HOW IT'S DONE

**1** Hold the disc in place with your left thumb. Bring the needle up through the fabric from the wrong side to the right side at Point A, reinserting it at Point B, before bringing it up again at Point C, down again at Point D and out again at Point E.

**2** Pass the needle over and around the first stitch, and then over and around the second stitch in the same way. Reinsert the needle at Point F.

**3** Bring the needle back up again at Point G. Pass it over and around the second stitch, and then over and around the first stitch, before reinserting the needle at Point H. You have now secured the disc with four stitches and can bring the needle up at Point I.

**4** With the working thread held loosely towards the left, pass the needle underneath the network of securing stitches and pull gently through.

**5** Reinsert the needle at Point J, bringing it out again at Point K, leaving the thread beneath the needle to form a chain stitch. Carefully pull the thread through.

**6** Pass the needle beneath the single securing stitch, keeping the thread to the left of the needle before gently pulling the thread through.

**7** Reinsert the needle at Point J. Create another chain stitch along the edge before bringing the needle out again at Point K. Repeat this sequence around the perimeter of the disc, carefully working the inner stitches across both threads where the securing stitches intersect.

**8** Secure the final chain stitch with a small, neat backstitch.

# Question 58:
# How do I use shaded satin stitch?

Shaded satin stitch is a highly effective way of adding dimension and depth to forms such as leaves or flower petals. Choose several closely related shades of the same colour for a subtle, naturalistic effect, or shades of varying colours for a livelier look.

To add depth to the shape you are filling, decide whether you want the darkest or lightest shade at the outer edge of your shape. You can make a group of shapes look very dimensional, simply by alternating this decision between the shapes, i.e. working some from light to dark, some from dark to light.

In a specific area of a shape, e.g. a petal, start at the centre of its outside edge. Starting at the centre will help to keep your stitches straight and parallel. Work satin stitches, alternating in length between long and short (this is called long and short stitch) from this central point towards the right of the shape until you reach the right-hand edge, then from the centre to the left-hand edge.

Continue around the whole flower or other shape, working each petal or other area in this first shade of long and short stitch, working each small area outwards from its centre as described.

Choose the shade closest in tone to the first shade worked. Work another row of stitches directly below the first row, making each stitch a long one. Continue until you have worked all of the row of stitches in this shade.

Continue to work rows of long stitches closely abutting the row above so that no fabric is visible between the stitches, using the next darkest, or lightest shade (depending whether you are working from light to dark, or vice versa), until you get to the last row of stitches needed to fill your shape.

Work the last row of stitches alternating in length, as you did with the first row, so that the shape is completely filled with stitches. If your shape tapers sharply to a point, you may need to omit some stitches to maintain a smooth result as you reach this point.

*RIGHT* Shaded satin stitch adds depth to simple flower shapes.

# Question 59:
# How do I work threaded herringbone stitch?

## HOW IT'S DONE

**1** Work a line of conventional herringbone stitch. Then select a blunt needle and a toning or contrasting thread for the extra stitch.

**2** Working from left to right, thread the top edge of the stitch as follows: bring the needle up through the fabric from the back to the front at Point A.

**3** Pass the needle under the topmost right arm of the first herringbone stitch and over the neighbouring left arm.

**4** Repeat this under-and-over weaving to the end of the line. Fasten off at Point B.

*BELOW* Threaded herringbone stitch combines geometry with softness.

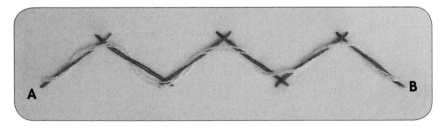

# Question 60:
# How do I work Vandyke stitch?

## HOW IT'S DONE

**1** Working from top to bottom, bring the needle up through the fabric from the wrong side to the right side at Point A.

**2** Reinsert at B. Bring the needle up again at C and down at D, creating a wide-bottomed cross-stitch.

**3** Bring the needle up again a small distance below A and wrap the thread under the crossed stitches from the right to the left without penetrating the fabric before inserting it again a small distance below Point D.

**4** Continue stitching and the wrapped stitches will create an effect like a backbone. This stitch, useful for creating leaf shapes, petals and wide borders, takes some practice to perfect, so be patient. Vandyke stitch works best with a heavy thread.

*RIGHT* Vandyke stitch is useful for borders and foliage effects.

# Question 61:
# How do I work buttonhole stitch?

This is a fun, quick to work and very versatile stitch.

There are some stitches for which it is not only possible to work without a frame or hoop, but which are actively more soothing to work in this way when you are accustomed to tensioning the fabric in your hand. This works best with a firm material, taking care to keep the stitches even yet relaxed. For example, in the nineteenth century, when many household linens were scallop edged with buttonhole stitch, the fabric was stabilised by being basted (tacked) to a firm yet flexible temporary backing fabric.

Flexible plastic is an ideal contemporary alternative to the oilcloth often used historically. If you would like to try out this method yourself simply cut away the basting stitches and remove the backing fabric when all the scallops have been worked (see page 104, question 89 for how to create a scalloped edge).

## HOW IT'S DONE

**1** Bring the needle through the fabric from the wrong side to the right side at Point A and insert again at B.

**2** Hold a loop of thread above the fabric as you pull the needle through, then bring the needle up again at C, keeping the loop of thread below the needle before pulling it tight enough to make a stitch that sits neatly.

**3** Repeat, working the stitches as close together or wide apart as you wish. This stitch is often worked in a circle like a wheel, with the loops forming the outer rim and the arms of the stitch forming the spokes.

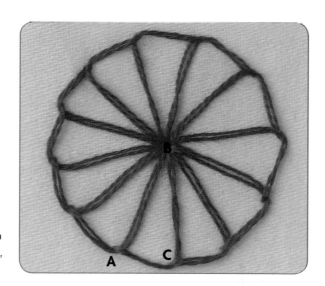

*RIGHT* Buttonhole stitch can be worked in a wheel, as shown here, or in a line.

# Question 62:
# What is knotted buttonhole stitch?

This stitch is worked like normal buttonhole stitch, except that before the needle is reinserted into the fabric, the thread is wrapped once around the needle, creating a decorative knot that sits at the end of the blanket/buttonhole stitch arm. Keep the thread taut as you pull the needle through, holding the wrapped thread in place with your thumb until it forms a knot that sits neatly on the surface of the fabric (see page 102, question 87 for Antwerp edging).

Knotted buttonhole stitch is perfect for depicting flower stamens at the heart of a floral design. The key to perfectly worked knotted buttonhole stitch is to tighten the stitch carefully before pulling the thread through, and always making sure that you pull the thread down towards yourself.

## EXPERT TIP
**66 You can create great spontaneity in knotted buttonhole stitch simply by changing the lengths of the arms. 99**

# Question 63:
## How do I work split stitch?

Working from left to right, bring the needle up through the fabric, from the wrong side to the right side, at Point A, the start of your sewing line. Take the needle back down through the fabric a short distance along your sewing line at Point B, making a basic stitch. Bring the needle back up again halfway along the first stitch at Point C ensuring that the needle goes through the thread, splitting it in two. Carry on stitching in this way.

*BELOW* Split stitch worked in straight and undulating lines.

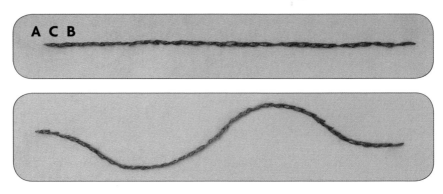

# Question 64:
## How can I use split stitch?

Split stitch is a very useful stitch for creating curved or straight lines and outlines. It is fast and simple to work. Split stitch may also be worked in closely worked rows as a filling stitch, giving a dense, smooth appearance. Using a soft, untwisted thread is advisable for best results.

Split stitch very closely resembles chain stitch, but is actually much finer. Worked as a delicate filling stitch, it was often used for stitching faces and hands in the *opus anglicanum* (literally, English work), mainly ecclesiastical work of the Middle Ages.

The split stitch was often worked in a spiral pattern to give a raised, three-dimensional effect.

**More Complex Stitches**

# 5
# RAISED STITCHES

These stitches are popular with freeform embroiderers, as they represent a diverse array of textures and subjects. These stitches are quick and enjoyable to work, so it is well worth practising them until they become second nature to you.

# Question 65:
# What is the difference between colonial and French knots?

The colonial knot is slightly larger and higher than a French knot. In working the French knot, the thread is wrapped around the needle in a single direction, while in the colonial knot the thread is taken in a figure of eight around the needle. French knots pull out more easily than colonial knots.

Stitchers who find French knots difficult to work sometimes prefer the colonial knot, so it is worth experimenting with both to see which suits you best. This simple-to-work stitch is also known as the candlewicking knot and is often used,

stitched close together, to form the lines within a candlewicking design.

Both stitches are detached knots, as opposed to those worked in continuous rows. Knot-type stitches worked in rows, such as double, or single-knot stitch, (also known as Antwerp edging, see page 102, question 87) are more resilient in wear and laundering than detached knot stitches, so are more suitable for frequently washed items or those that need to withstand heavy use.

## EXPERT TIP

66 **Both types of knot are definitely best worked on fabric tensioned in a hoop.** 99

# Question 66:
# How do I work a colonial knot?

Bring the needle up through the
fabric from the wrong side to the
right side, at the point that you
want to create a knot. Holding the
thread firmly with one hand, wind
the thread round the needle in a
figure of eight before reinserting the
needle close to where the thread
first emerged. Keeping the thread
held taut, carefully draw the thread
through the fabric, leaving the knot
sitting neatly on the surface.

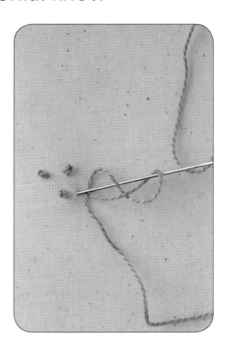

*RIGHT* Working the colonial knot. Here
you can clearly see its distinctive figure
of eight formation.

# Question 67:
# How do I work a French knot?

Bring the needle up through the fabric from the wrong side to the right side, at the point that you want to create a knot, Point A.

Holding the thread firmly with one hand, wrap it around the needle twice before reinserting the needle close to Point A. Keeping the thread held taut, and holding the knot in place to stabilise it, carefully draw the thread through the fabric, leaving the twists you have created sitting neatly on the surface.

## EXPERT TIP

66 **Working French knots in a spiral pattern, using a graduated thread, creates a lively design in no time at all.** 99

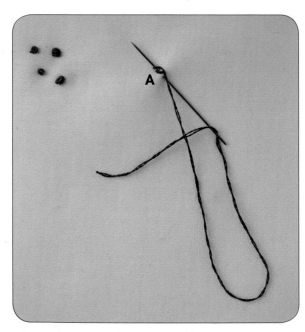

*LEFT* Working the French knot, which can have a varying number of wraps depending on your desired effect.

# Question 68:
## How do I work a bullion knot?

Bring the needle up through the fabric from the wrong side to the right side at Point A. Reinsert the needle at Point B and pull through, leaving a long loop of thread. Bring the tip of the needle up again at Point A. With the needle still in the fabric, wrap the thread around the point of the needle five to eight times. Carefully holding the wrap between the finger and thumb of your left hand, pull the needle

through the wrapping. Pack down the twists you have just formed, towards where the thread emerged from the fabric at Point A, using the top of the needle. Reinsert the needle at Point B so that the wrapped thread lies neatly along the fabric between Points A and B.

*BELOW* Wrapping the twists securely around the needle produces a neat, well-formed bullion stitch.

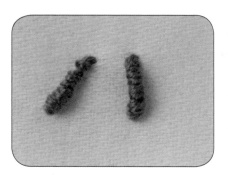
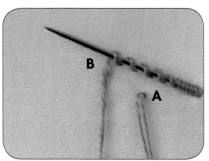

# Question 69:
## How do I work zigzag chain stitch?

Many freestyle embroidery stitches are richly textural and can be used to create very decorative effects. A good example is the twisted zigzag

chain stitch. This stitch often used for borders gives a rich, braided look. Once you are proficient in this stitch, it is quick to work, but it is well worth practising on some spare fabric to familarise yourself with the technique. It is a good idea to draw three evenly spaced, parallel guidelines on your fabric. The design will look different according to the spacing of the lines – approximately 5mm (¼in) apart is a good distance for learning the stitch.

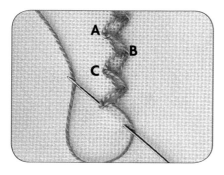

## HOW IT'S DONE

To work zigzag chain stitch:

**1** Work from the top towards the bottom of the area you want to stitch.

**2** Bring the needle up through the fabric from the wrong side to the right side at Point A on the left hand guideline.

**3** Loop and hold the thread down toward the left and reinsert the needle at Point A, bringing it out again at Point B, on the right hand guideline.

**4** Carefully pull through before making another chain stitch down and towards the left hand guideline in the same way, by reinserting the needle inside the loop at Point B.

**5** Bring the needle out again at Point C, keeping the thread looped under the needle before pulling through gently.

**6** Continue making these alternating stitches approximately 5mm (¼in)apart down the line, or scaled according to the width of your drawn line.

**7** Secure the last loop with a small stitch as for regular chain stitch.

# Question 70:
# How do I make clusters of raised stitches to create a pattern?

Knotted stitches add greatly to the texture of a piece of freeform embroidery. Generally, this term is used to describe stitches in which loops of thread are passed around the needle before it enters the fabric, leaving decorative loops of thread in place on the surface of the fabric. Working a number of knotted stitches close to each other creates a sculptural surface relatively quickly, ideal for suggesting landscape, foliage, or animal life, depending on the scale of thread and stitch used.

*BELOW* Bullion knots worked closely produce a three-dimensional-looking chrysanthemum.

# Question 71:
# How do I start and finish off these raised stitches?

Since individual knot stitches do not form a line suitable for enclosing the thread at the rear of the work, you will need to begin and end your stitching using the away waste knot method, as described in question 19.

The waste backstitch method is also suitable for starting these detached knot stitches. To work a waste backstitch start to your detached knot work, simply begin a line of backstitch, working from the front of the fabric towards the back, roughly 3cm (1¼in) away from where you want your first knot to be. Leave a tail approximately 5cm (2in) long on the surface of the fabric. When you have finished your desired detached knots, unpick the backstitches before running in the tail through the reverse of the first few knots.

# 6
# WHEELS AND WEBS

There is something very therapeutic about working circles in embroidery. These delightfully tactile shapes are soothing to work, and can represent everything from fruit to flowers, wheels to trees. Enjoy!

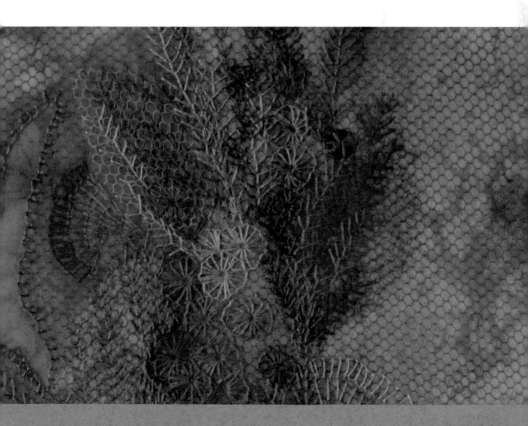

# Question 72:
# How do I make a stem stitch wheel?

Stem stitch is also known as a whipped wheel. Lay a foundation of straight stitches of even length radiating outwards from a central point. You can use any number of stitches, but six is a good number to practise with.

*BELOW* Stem stitch wheels are very soothing to stitch.

# Question 73:
# How do I make a spider's web (woven wheel)?

To create the basic structure of the web, sew an odd number of straight stitches radiating outwards from the centre of a circle. Five spokes makes a good starting point for this stitch. Bring the needle up near the centre of the circle. Working clockwise, take the needle and thread over the first line and under the next, leaving the thread on the surface of the fabric rather than penetrating it. Take care to keep the tension of the thread even as you weave. Continue needle weaving around the circle until the web has been filled.

## EXPERT TIP

66 **Using a blunt-ended needle for the needleweaving means that the threads do not get snagged as you work.** 99

*BELOW* A spider's web worked in stranded cotton.

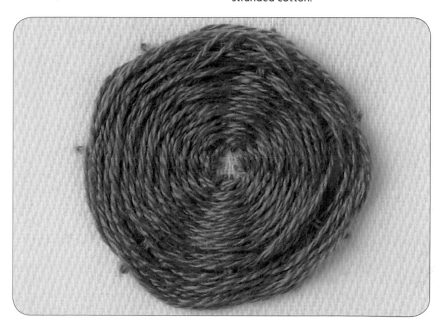

# Question 74:
# What is the difference between woven and whipped circles?

In a woven circle, the weaving thread is literally woven in and out of the foundation stitches. In a whipped circle, the thread is whipped, also sometimes described as being wrapped, around the foundation thread prior to being taken underneath, rather than over and under the foundation threads.

In both types of circular designs, the stitches are worked in an outwards radiating way, as for the spider's web, and can be worked on any number of base straight stitches, odd or even, unlike the spider's web, which needs an odd number of foundation threads.

BELOW Whipped (left) and woven (right) wheels are versatile and fun to work with.

# Question 75:
## How do I work needle weaving?

Needle weaving is worked with a blunt needle so that the supporting threads are not pierced and shredded. The blunt needle glides around the foundation threads, making the stitching pleasant to work and producing a smooth result.

# Question 76:
## What patterns can I create with wheels and circles?

Wheels and circles are very versatile shapes and are fun to work. They are ideal for creating flowers, flower centres and polka dots. You could also use them to suggest trees, wheels, shells or stones. The foundation stitches, i.e. the spokes, can be worked in the same colour as the weaving stitch, a closely toning colour, or a completely different one, depending on what effect you wish to achieve.

## EXPERT TIP

66 Using ribbon for the needle weaving instead of thread produces a rose-like result. Allow the ribbon to fall naturally into petal shapes rather than pulling it tight. 99

# 7

# COUCHING STITCHES

As soon as you start freeform embroidery, you will fall in love with the wide array of yarns, ribbons, laces and cords available. Couching offers you a simple and decorative method of incorporating these exciting materials into your work.

# Question 77:
## What is pendant couching stitch?

In pendant couching, also known as loop couching, the laid thread, ribbon or yarn is looped, pendant-like, before being secured to the ground fabric. In open loop pendant couching, the couched thread is laid in an undulating wave pattern rather than in closed loops.

# Question 78:
## How do I work pendant couching stitch?

Pendant couching offers many opportunities for experimentation.

### HOW IT'S DONE

**1** For classic pendant couching, bring the thread to be laid up through the fabric from the wrong side to the right.

**2** With your couching thread, make a small securing stitch from Points A to B.

**3** Allowing the thread to be laid to fall into natural, closed loops, in a line, make a small tying stitch over the double thread at the top of each loop.

**4** To work open loop pendant couching, let the laid thread fall into a wave pattern rather than closed loops.

**5** Add a small tying stitch at the top of each wave. For both types of stitch, take the laid thread down through the fabric to the reverse side and secure it with small stitches.

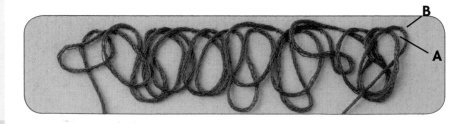

# Question 79:
## What is scale couching?

Scale couching may be worked as a single, wavy, couched line or in multiple, closely placed lines as an open filling stitch. The latter produces a classic 'fish scale' appearance (see bottom picture).

# Question 80:
## How do I work scale couching?

**HOW IT'S DONE**

**1** Bring the thread to be laid up at Point A.

**2** Bring the tying thread up just beside it and then down again over it to secure.

**3** Arrange the thread to be couched in a curved shape across the fabric.

**4** Bring needle up at Point A and insert it again at Point B, securing the start of the couched thread. Then bring the needle up again at Point C and, laying the thread over the couched thread, reinsert it at Point D.

**5** Carry on taking small stitches over the waved thread holding the curve of the laid thread in place. If working as a filling stitch, continue placing the laid threads and securing them with tying stitches so that the rows touch each other, alternating to form the fish scale design.

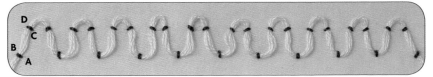

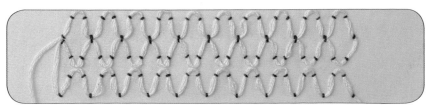

# Question 81:
# How do I create an outline with couching stitch?

Couching is ideal for creating bold, unbroken outlines as you are free to use a thread, yarn, ribbon or indeed a more unusual material such as leather or metallics to create a strong line, rather than being restricted to materials which are easy to stitch and can be pulled back and forth through the fabric. The couched, laid thread literally sits upon the surface of the fabric, creating a solid line. Couching is quick, simple and fun to work.

Measure out enough thread or yarn to cover your outline, plus a little extra for starting and finishing off. For added drama and dimension, couched lines may be padded for a very rich result. Various materials can be used. String is an excellent choice, as it is flexible enough to create even, tightly curved lines.

First, secure the string to the surface of the fabric using regular sewing thread, worked in small stitches. Arrange the string as desired — singly or in a pattern. For a glittering finish, cover the string with cut lengths of bullion (a hollow centred spring-like coiled wire widely used in goldwork). Having cut the bullion according to

## HOW IT'S DONE

**1** Measure out enough thread or yarn to cover your outline, plus a little extra for starting and finishing off.

**2** Bring the thread to be laid up at the start of the line. If you are using a heavy thread, such as a metallic rope, you will need to use the plunging method described in the answer to question 50 to get the bulky "rope" through the fabric and secure it.

**3** On the front of your fabric, follow the outline of your design with the laid rope, securing it with small, carefully tensioned stitches spaced so as to hold the outline in your desired shape. You may, of course, choose to embellish the couched rope or yarn further with more prominent stitches as well as these securing ones.

**4** End your stitching on the rear of the fabric with the same plunging method.

the width of the string at a slanted angle, secure it across the string at this angle by threading the bullion as you would a bugle bead (see page 178, question 162 How do I attach a bugle bead?, following the directions for sewing on a bugle bead so it lies flat). Continue placing cut lengths of bullion until the string is enclosed.

# Question 82:
# How do I decorate couching stitches?

Couched threads can be secured with small, discreet stitches in colours that blend imperceptibly with the laid threads, or can be embellished in a wide variety of ways either by having the securing stitches worked in dramatically different colours and textures, or by being whipped with boldly contrasting shades and weights of yarn. A wide variety of stitches are suitable for this, including blanket stitch, rosette chain stitch and herringbone stitch. As with all freeform embroidery, experimentation is the key to both enjoyment and success.

Bricking in a contrast colour is a great way to build up a richly dimensional border in couching. It looks sumptuous and much more labour intensive than it actually is to achieve. In bricking, lines of couching are worked horizontally across the desired area. It is easiest to work from top to bottom when applying these. Make the securing stitches in an alternating 'brick' pattern with each stitch placed halfway between the stitch on the line above.

This type of couching is also known as 'or nué', or 'Italian shading' when the securing threads are coloured and/or spaced so as to colour the design from light to dark.

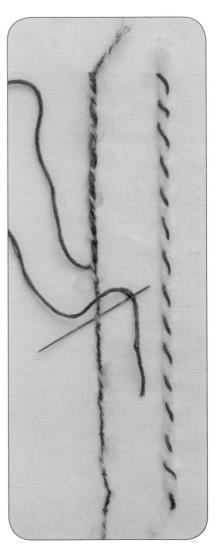

*ABOVE* Whipping couching stitches adds colour and texture quickly and simply.

# Question 83:
# How do I work Bokhara couching?

Work on a firmly stretched piece of fabric marked with parallel lines at regular intervals as shown, to help you keep the tying stitches even.

Couched stitches tied down at regular intervals by several little tight stitches, designed to form a pattern, becomes known as Bokhara stitch. Unlike regular couching, which often utilises contrasting thread, Bokhara couching uses only one thread, which forms both the laid and couching threads. This is known as 'self-couching'.

Bokhara couching is most usually worked as shown here, with a horizontal straight stitch couched down by tiny straight stitches worked in patterns.

Other types of self-couching techniques are Klosterstitch and Romanian couching, which are subtly different. In Klosterstitching, the couching thread is worked to be as invisible as possible, whereas in Romanian couching, the couching stitch is meant to work back into the design to produce a textured, but not visually intrusive, difference.

All types of Bokhara couching stitches produce a pattern that is highly reminiscent of a woven textile.

## HOW IT'S DONE

**1** Lay a long, straight stitch in the area to be filled, starting at the bottom left-hand corner of the shape at Point A and taking the needle back down through the fabric again at Point B. Do not pull this laid stitch too tightly; it will be adequately secured by the subsequent tying stitches.

**2** Bring the needle up again at Point C, and back down through the fabric again at Point D, making a small, firm, diagonal tying stitch across the laid thread. Bring the needle back up again at Point E, and down again at Point F.

**3** Continue making these tying stitches as required along the laid thread.

**4** Bring the needle up at Point G, just above Point A, to place the next long laid thread. Make tying stitches along this laid thread, as before. Continue placing laying threads from left to right. Add tying stitches as before, until the entire shape has been filled. There should be no ground fabric visible between the laid threads.

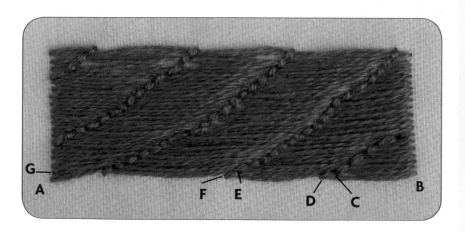

*ABOVE* Bokhara couching is a dense filling stitch.

# 8

# EDGING STITCHES

Edging stitches perform two functions. They finish off raw edges, but can also be highly decorative in their own right. Quick and fun to work, they are well worth learning and will soon become second nature to stitch.

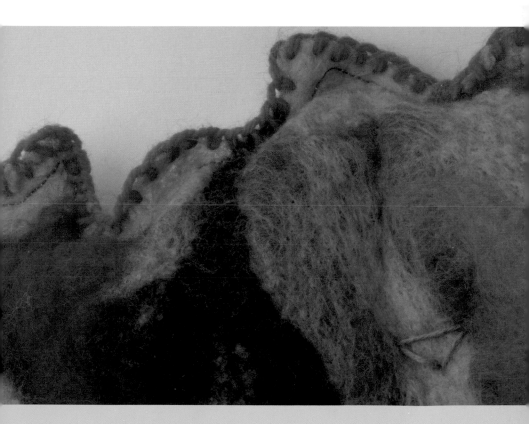

# Question 84:
## How do I hem fabric?

Hemming is the action of securing the edge of a piece of fabric in order to prevent it from fraying. This is generally achieved by turning and pressing under the edge of the fabric and stitching it in place to make the fold permanent. Alternatively, the fabric may be attached to an edging of some sort, for example bias binding, a braid, or crocheted edging.

### EXPERT TIP

66 Very fine fabrics and delicate projects, such as cotton lawn lingerie or baby clothes, benefit from rolled, rather than folded, hems. These are soft and comfortable to wear. 99

# Question 85:
## What decorative stitches can be used to hem fabric?

There are a number of simple stitches that can be used to hem fabric. Blanket stitch is a popular and quickly worked choice. Buttonhole stitch, worked on a straight or scalloped edge, is also a well-loved hemming stitch, as are zigzag and herringbone stitch. If using zigzag stitch to hem, make every fourth stitch or so a backstitch in order to strengthen the hem.

### EXPERT TIP

66 Shell hemming stitch is easily worked and is perfect for lingerie. Make a running stitch hem, interspersed regularly with two stitches over and across the hem. Pull the fabric up into shell shapes between each group of running stitches as you work. 99

# Question 86:
## How do I work blanket stitch?

### HOW IT'S DONE

**1** Working from left to right, bring the needle up through the fabric from the wrong side to the right side at Point A and insert again at B.

**2** Hold a loop of thread above the fabric as you pull the needle through, then bring the needle up again at C, keeping the loop of thread below the needle before pulling it tight enough to make a stitch that sits neatly. Repeat, working stitches as close together or spaced out as you wish.

**3** Varying the lengths of the arms of the blanket stitch creates a dynamic effect. When the stitch is worked on the surface of the fabric rather than as an edging, it is known as buttonhole stitch.

*BELOW* Blanket stitch edges and decorates simultaneously.

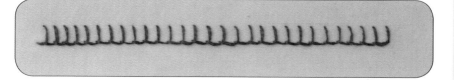

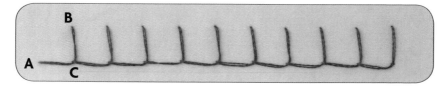

# Question 87:
## How do I work Antwerp edging?

Working from left to right, bring your needle up through the fabric from the wrong side towards the right at Point A.

Reinsert your needle at Point B as shown and with the thread held beneath the tip of the needle, pull through leaving a loop of thread as if you are working a blanket stitch.

Insert your needle inside the loop of thread you have just created.

Holding the thread beneath your needle, pull through gently to form a knot.

Continue working to form a line of stitches, which could be used either as an edging or on the surface of the fabric.

*BELOW* Antwerp edging has a subtle twist at the base of each stitch.

# Question 88:
# How do I work buttonhole with picot stitch?

Work as normal buttonhole stitch up to the point where you want to create your first picot. At this point, wind the thread three times around the tip of the needle at the same kind of tension you would use for a French knot.

Holding the wraps in place with your left thumb, carefully pull the needle through to form a picot.

Pass the needle through the buttonhole stitch that lies above, working from the left towards the right without piercing the fabric. This begins the next buttonhole stitch.

Continue to work picots on the buttonhole stitches spaced as required.

*BELOW* An illustration showing how to work buttonhole with picot.

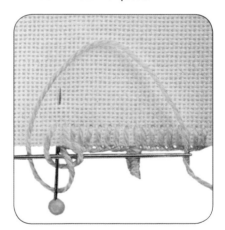

*BELOW* Buttonhole with picot has a knotted edge.

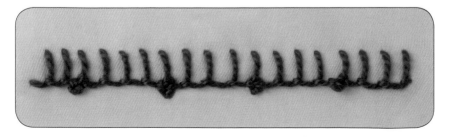

# Question 89:
# How do I create a scalloped edge?

Draw a line parallel with and approximately 1.5cm (½in) in from the end of the fabric on which you wish to work the scalloped edge.

Using a coin roughly 1.5cm (½in) across as a pattern, or any other template to suit your desired scallop size, draw the scallops so that the bottoms are even with this line.

Stitch around the scallops using buttonhole stitch. This is essentially blanket stitch worked very closely together so that no fabric is visible between the stitches.

When the stitching is complete, cut the excess fabric away from the scalloped edge, taking great care not to snip the stitching.

For a more pronounced effect, you can lay a thick cotton thread along the scalloped edge and secure it with a few stitches before you begin buttonholing over it. This gives a rich, raised look.

*BELOW* Scalloped edges add a delicate, nostalgic charm to a finished piece.

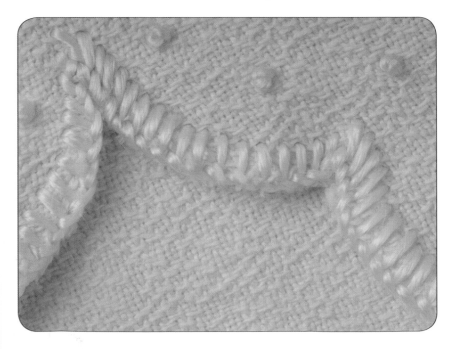

# 9

# CABLE AND LINKED STITCHES

This group of stitches is useful for creating outlines and borders. Some stitches are more tricky to master than others, but produce such satisfyingly rich results that it is worth persevering with learning them.

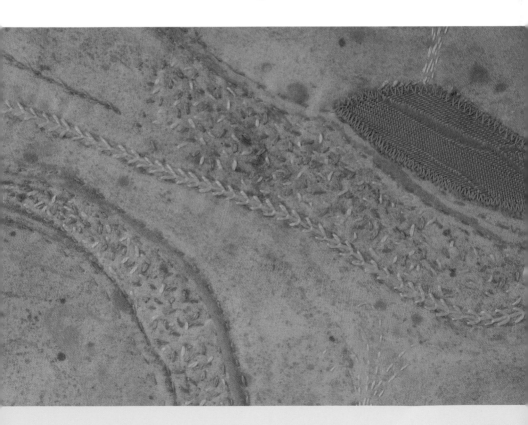

# Question 90:
## What is cable stitch?

Cable stitch is also known as side-to-side stem stitch or alternate stem stitch. It produces a solid-looking line of stitches that can be worked as a single line or in several rows.

# Question 91:
## When is cable stitch used?

Cable stitch is traditionally used to prepare fabric for smocking. Pulled up, it gathers fabric into pleats. You can use it in this way on your ground fabric, or a piece of material applied to your ground fabric, for added textural interest.

# Question 92:
## How do I work cable stitch?

For even results, mark out a straight line on your fabric. Working from left to right, bring the needle up through the fabric from the wrong side to the right side at Point A, before taking a small stitch from Points B to C. Make sure you bring the needle out below the working thread as you stitch. Take a small stitch from Point D to Point E, this time bringing out the needle above the working thread. Continue making these two stitches to the right.

Cable stitch is often used as the top row of stitching on smocked garments because it is a tight, stable line of close stitches. You can utilise the same qualities to create, secure, or define a particular area of fabric. Leave the stitches flat, or pull them up to create the characteristic 'tubes' of smocking.

You could then apply this piece of smocked fabric to your ground fabric, creating a great deal of surface interest and dimensionality (see Appliqué Techniques Chapter 14, starting page 187, for details on how to affix one layer of material to another for decorative effect).

If you are going to use rows of cable stitch to produce a smocked piece of fabric, to achieve a regular, neat, traditionally smocked result, you will need to use a lightweight fabric such as cotton. Make the width of this two to three times your desired finished fabric width.

Heat-transferred smocking grids of iron-on dot markings are available if you become interested in incorporating smocking into your work, but are not necessary for initial experimentation. Mark the fabric with dots on the wrong side of the fabric, making the space between the dots 8mm (¼in). Make the space between the rows of dots 12mm (½in). Increase the space between the dots if you prefer a less pronounced gather.

To pre-gather the fabric, starting on the right side of the fabric, sew a row of running stitch across the fabric, with the visible part of the stitch over, not through, the dots. At the end of the row, leave a thread end approximately 10cm (4in) long. Repeat this on every row, loosely tying the tails together when all rows are finished.

Now you can begin to smock, using cable stitch. Bring the needle up at the left side of the first pre-gathered pleat. Float the thread across until it is on the right side of the second pleat. Bring the needle up on the left side of the second pleat, float it across to the right side of the third pleat, and bring it up on the left side of the third pleat. Repeat this pattern across the row. At the end of the row, take the needle through to the wrong side of the fabric, and secure with a few small stitches worked over each other.

Of course, as with all freeform embroidery, you need not work smocking with this degree of accuracy. You could also work cable stitches and pull up the pleats more randomly for a wilder textural effect, either on an area of ground fabric, or a piece to be applied on top of the fabric (see Appliqué Techniques Chapter 14, starting page 187, also questions 182-184 on making and applying slips, in Chapter 15, begins page 195, 3D Embroidery Techniques).

*BELOW* Cable stitch can be used as a heavy outlining stitch, or gathered up when smocking.

# Question 93:
## What is cable chain stitch?

This stitch is useful for working borders. It resembles a heavy, linked metal chain. Cable chain can be useful in embroidered portraits for simulating bracelets and necklaces.

It also works well for depicting the wings of bees and other insects.

*BELOW* Cable chain stitch is a simple stitch to work.

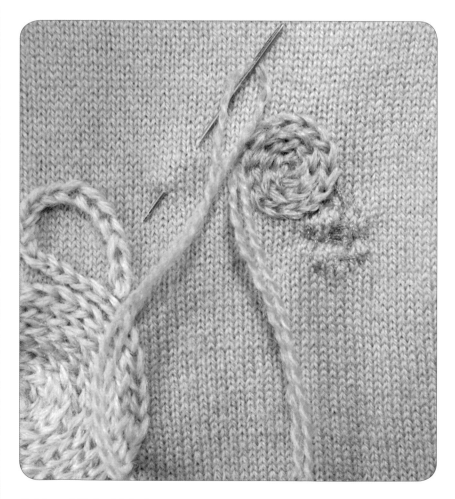

**Cable and Linked Stitches**

# Question 94:
## How is cable chain stitch worked?

### HOW IT'S DONE

**1** Work this stitch from top to bottom.

**2** Start with a regular chain stitch by bringing the needle up from the wrong side of the fabric to the right at Point A and reinserting it at Point A, forming a loop.

**3** Bring the needle up again at Point B, holding down the loop with the point of the needle.

**4** Twist the thread clockwise once around the needle and draw the twist in tight.

**5** Holding the thread down with your thumb, reinsert the needle at Point C, just outside the first chain stitch, and up again at Point D, inside the thread loop.

**6** Carefully pull the thread through. Continue to alternate chain and linking stitches in this way. Complete the final loop with a small stitch.

*RIGHT* Cable chain stitch is useful for depicting the chainlink it so closely resembles.

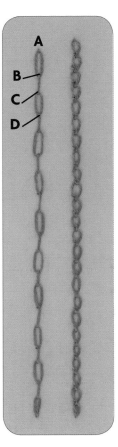

# Question 95:
## How can chain stitch be used as an outline?

Chain stitch is ideal for use as an outline as it travels smoothly around curved shapes and can also turn sharp corners. It is a fast-growing and simply worked stitch that is effective as a single line or massed together for emphasis. It can be worked in a zigzag formation that looks dynamic and playful, and can also be whipped for extra interest.

# Question 96:
## What is the difference between chain stitch and open chain stitch?

Regular chain stitch is formed from a series of loops, emerging from a single point in the preceding loop, giving this stitch its characteristic chain-like appearance.

Open chain stitch is formed from a series of loops, each of which emerges from two parallel points in the preceding loop, giving this stitch a ladder-like appearance.

### EXPERT TIP
66 When working any type of chain stitch, don't pull the thread too tightly, as this stitch is inclined to pucker fabric, especially when worked in curved lines. 99

# Question 97:
# How do you work open chain stitch?

Work this stitch from top to bottom. If you want to produce very regular stitching, mark your fabric with two parallel lines.

## HOW IT'S DONE

**1** Bring the needle up through the fabric from the wrong side to the right at Point A.

**2** Reinsert the needle at Point B. Bring it up through the fabric again at Point C, looping the thread beneath the point of the needle and keeping the tension fairly loose.

**3** Reinsert the needle at Point D and bring it up again at Point E, again with a loop of thread beneath the point of the needle.

**4** Repeat until the line of open chain stitch reaches your required length.

**5** To secure the final loop, make a small stitch at each lower corner of the loop.

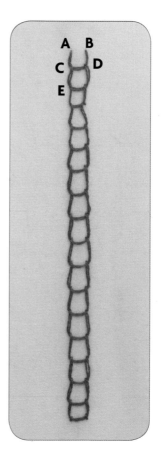

# Question 98:
## How do I work rosette chain stitch?

Rosette chain stitch is a richly textured stitch, also known as bead edging. Worked in a line, it is used to form edgings and borders. Worked in a circular or oval shape, it creates attractive floral motifs.

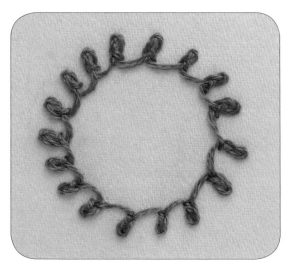

*BELOW* Rosette chain stitch worked in a line and a circle.

## HOW IT'S DONE

**1** To make the stitch form a line, work from right to left. If you want perfect, evenly sized stitches, mark the fabric with two parallel lines.

**2** Bring the needle up through the fabric from the wrong side to the right at Point A.

**3** Make a twisted loop with the thread towards the left, holding the loop down with your thumb.

**4** Reinsert the needle at Point B and bring it up again at Point C inside the twisted loop, slanting the needle back towards the right.

**5** Pull the thread through. Without penetrating the fabric, pass the needle up under the top thread.

**6** Loop the thread as before, then take the needle back down through the fabric at Point D to start the next stitch.

**7** Bring the needle up again at Point E and repeat.

# Question 99:
# What is fern stitch?

Fern stitch is a simply worked stitch consisting of three straight stitches worked in a fan shape. The stitch lends itself perfectly to suggesting foliage stems and grassy landscapes. The three stitches can be of equal or varied length and the angles between them can be equal or different, depending on the effect required.

*ABOVE* As its name suggest, fern stitch is perfect for depicting foliage.

# Question 100:
# How do I link fern stitch?

Fern stitch works very well to create naturalistic, branching stems of foliage.

## HOW IT'S DONE

**1** To work fern stitch in this way, mark where you wish the base of your stem to be.

**2** Bring the needle up through the fabric from the wrong side to the right side at Point A and pull the thread through.

**3** Reinsert the needle at Point B, bring out again at Point C, and pull the thread through.

**4** Reinsert the needle at Point B, bring the needle out again at Point D, and pull the thread through.

**5** Reinsert the needle at Point B, bring it out again at Point E, and then fully pull the thread through.

**6** Once more, insert the needle at Point A. Bring the needle out again at Point F and pull the thread through. Reinsert the needle at Point A, come out again at Point G. reinsert at Point A and continue in this way until your line of linked fern stitch achieves the desired length.

*RIGHT* Linked fern stitch is perfect for depicting foliage, as seen here.

# Question 101:
# How do I work feathered chain stitch?

## HOW IT'S DONE

**1** Working from top to bottom, bring the needle up through the fabric from the wrong side to the right at Point A.

**2** Reinsert it at the same place, bringing it up and out again at Point B, just to the left below the needle point, keeping the loop of thread held under the tip of the needle. Gently pull through.

**3** Insert the needle at Point C, making sure that Points A, B and C make a straight line.

**4** Bring the needle up and out again at Point D, level with Point B. Reinsert the needle at Point D, bringing it up again at Point C, holding the thread looped beneath the needle point.

**5** Gently pull through. Reinsert the needle at Point E, making sure that Points D, C and E make a straight line.

**6** Bring the needle out again at Point F, level with Point C. This begins the next repeat. Continue making these long-tailed chain stitches, alternating left and right to create a feathered pattern. Fasten off the last chain stitch with a small securing stitch.

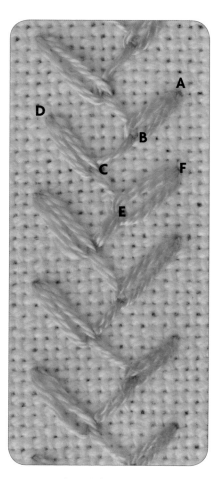

*ABOVE* Feathered chain stitch produces a simple but lively border.

# Question 102:
# What is Cretan stitch?

Cretan stitch is a criss-crossing, interlaced stitch from the fly and feather group of stitches. It may be worked from top to bottom or from left to right. The basic stitch is worked in parallel rows, but it can also be used to fill shapes.

Knowledge of a history of embroidery in Crete dates at least back to the time of the writing of *The Odyssey,* believed to have been written around the 11th century BC. Cretan stitch features widely on skirts and jackets; the patterns passed down through the ages and seen on designs in frescoes in the palace of Minos at Knossos, which dates from approximately 500BC.

*BELOW* Cretan stitch worked irregularly.

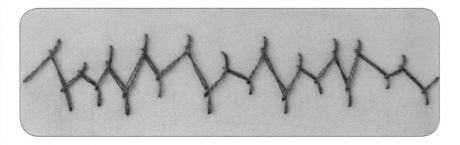

# Question 103:
# When is Cretan stitch used?

Cretan stitch lends itself perfectly to stitching petals and leaves since it outlines the shape and fills it at the same time. It is an organic-looking stitch with lots of surface interest and looks especially naturalistic when two shades of thread are used together in the needle.

*ABOVE* Cretan stitch produces authentic foliage shapes quickly and easily.

# Question 104:
## How do I work Cretan stitch?

**HOW IT'S DONE**

**1** Bring the needle up through the fabric from the wrong side to the right side at Point A and pull the thread through.

**2** Reinsert the needle at Point B, bringing it up out again at Point C, holding the thread beneath the needle tip while carefully pulling through.

**3** Insert the needle at Point D, bringing it up again at Point E, holding the thread beneath the needle tip.

**4** Gently pull the thread through. Continue towards the left.

**5** You may find it helpful to mark four faint parallel lines on your fabric while you are practising this stitch.

If you are working as a leaf shape, start at the leaf tip and work downwards.

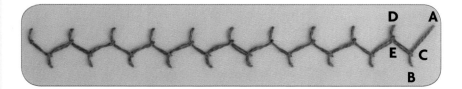

*ABOVE* Cretan stitch worked regularly.

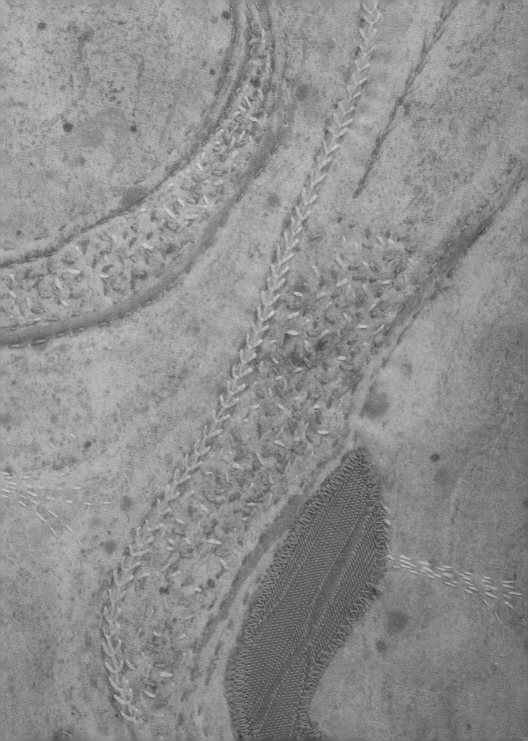

# Question 105:
## When is open Cretan stitch used?

Open Cretan stitch is often used to create borders. It is worked, as its name suggests, with space between the stitches, giving it an open, airy appearance.

*RIGHT* Open Cretan stitch worked randomly on a hand-dyed background to dramatic effect.

# Question 106:
## How do I work open Cretan stitch?

### HOW IT'S DONE

**1** Working from right to left, work as for regular Cretan stitch.

**2** Ensure that the needle always points from the outside of the border towards the inside, passing over the thread each time to form a loop.

**3** Multiple rows of this stitch worked in graduating tones of the same colour look very effective.

**4** Criss-crossing rows in contrasting or toning shades make a dynamic, quickly worked border.

### EXPERT TIP

66 **Open Cretan stitch lends itself well to working around gently curved shapes.** 99

# Question 107:
## What is chevron stitch?

Chevron stitch is a zigzagging stitch that is topped and tailed by horizontal stitches.

A chevron is a V-shaped pattern or triangular shape pointing up, but more usually, down. As a strong, instantly recognisable graphic shape, it is widely used in insignia, heraldry, traffic signs, flag design and buildings. In architecture, a chevron is a rafter or beam, or the shape made where two beams meet at an angle at the roof. In embroidery, chevron stitch is similarly used where a clean, strong look is required.

Working chevron in rows as a filling stitch can yield interesting results if you vary the spacings between the rows. Also, adding a double backstitch (see page 50, question 46) in the centre of some of the diamonds formed by the chevrons makes a simple, yet effective visual punctuation.

# Question 108:
## When is chevron stitch used?

Chevron stitch is ideal for producing neat, decorative borders with a clean, graphic look.

*BELOW* Worked in a variegated thread adds dynamism to chevron stitch.

### EXPERT TIP
66 **Work rows of chevron stitch closely together to produce a lattice-effect filling stitch.** 99

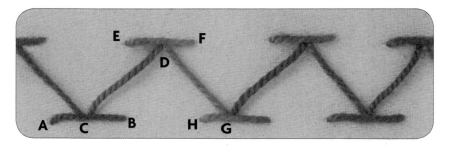

# Question 109:
# How is chevron stitch worked?

## HOW IT'S DONE

**1** Working from left to right, bring the needle up through the fabric from the wrong side to the right at Point A.

**2** Reinsert it at Point B and bring it back up again at Point C above the centre of the stitch you have just made.

**3** Take the needle back down again at Point D on the upper line, above and to the right of Point B.

**4** Bring the needle up again at Point E. Reinsert the needle at Point F and bring it up again at Point D just below the centre of the stitch you have just made.

**5** Take the needle back down again at Point G and bring it up again at Point H. Continue in this way if it is important that the border is uniform.

You might find it helpful to mark faint parallel guidelines before stitching.

# Question 110:
# What is fishbone stitch?

Fishbone stitch is a filling stitch with a distinctive fishbone appearance. It is useful for simultaneously creating a shape and filling it.

The stitch has a distinctive rib like formation in the centre of the pattern. This makes it especially helpful for depicting a realistic leaf shape or for representing feathers. As this is such a versatile stitch, it is well worth experimenting with working it in differing scales and levels of openness, so that with just this single stitch, you are able to embroider a wide range of foliage and feathery shapes. You can make the shapes as light and airily spaced or tight and close as you wish.

# Question 111:
# How do I work fishbone stitch?

## HOW IT'S DONE

**1** Draw out a leaf shape on your fabric, and mark in a central line.

**2** Working from the tip of your shape towards its base, bring the needle up through the fabric from the wrong side to the right at Point A and take it down again at Point B.

**3** Bring the needle up again at Point C and take it down again at Point D so that the previous stitch is just overlapped. Bring the needle out again at Point E.

**4** Reinsert the needle at Point F, overlapping the previous stitch. Bring the needle up again at Point G, ready to commence the next pair of stitches.

**5** Continue to make alternating stitches left and right. The stitches should overlap each other along your marked centre line, or wherever you wish to imply a strong, central vein. This line can be curved or straight to suit your design.

*RIGHT* Fishbone stitch is useful for producing leaf shapes, as pictured.

# 10

# FILLING STITCHES

Necessary for filling in defined areas and representing backgrounds, these stitches offer an array of textures and patterns, some of which can cover a lot of ground quickly.

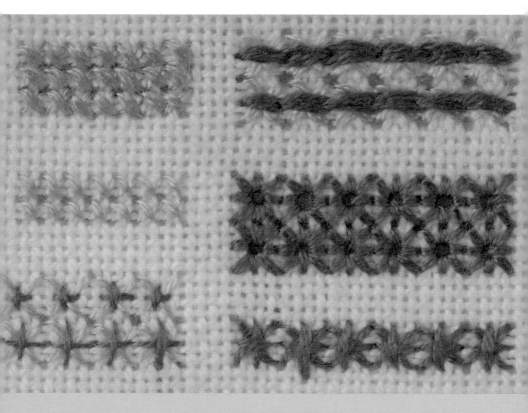

# Question 112:
## What are filling stitches?

Filling stitches are worked, as their name suggests, specifically to fill a space. They may be worked together, as in the case of laid filling stitches, or as single stitches massed to form a group. Laid filling stitches consist of threads laid over the fabric's surface and secured using any of a variety of couching methods. Individual stitches often used for filling shapes include fly stitch and star stitch, but in freeform embroidery, you can choose literally any stitch and use it as a filling, either in a geometric, tessellated arrangement or worked randomly within a shape.

# Question 113:
## How do I work buttonhole filling stitch?

If you want your lines of buttonhole filling to be neat and even, you may find it useful to mark some parallel horizontal lines on your fabric.

It is well worth taking the time to produce a sampler of filling stitches; both as a practice piece and as a guide to refer to when creating new works. Make yourself a paper guide to the stitches worked and write on the names of the stitches, and any notes on how they were made, such as if a particular thread worked especially well, or badly, and keep this close by the actual sampler. An example of a filling stitch sampler opens this chapter on page 127.

### EXPERT TIP
**66 Buttonhole filling gives an airy look perfect for depicting lace or other open structured materials. 99**

*OPPOSITE PAGE* Buttonhole filling is a useful, quickly worked, open filling stitch.

## HOW IT'S DONE

**1** Work the stitch from the top of the shape you are filling towards the bottom.

**2** Starting at the top left of the shape, bring the needle up through the fabric from the wrong side towards the right at Point A.

**3** Reinsert the needle at Point B and bring it up again at Point C, holding the thread beneath the needle to produce a buttonhole stitch.

**4** Gently pull through. Make another buttonhole stitch alongside this first one and then, slightly further along, make another pair of buttonhole stitches.

**4** Continue until you have completed a row of stitches, then work the second line of stitches from right to left. Bring the needle up through the fabric from the wrong side to the right at Point D.

**5** Reinsert the needle at Point E, just above the existing stitch, and bring it out again at Point F, holding the thread beneath the tip of the needle to form a loop.

**6** Gently pull through. Make a second buttonhole stitch alongside in the same way, and continue to make pairs of buttonhole stitches along this new line.

**7** Place each pair of buttonhole stitches in the large loop formed between each pair of stitches in the line above. Work the third line of stitches from left to right, in the same way. Continue until your shape has been filled. If you wish you may work the groups of stitches in clusters of three or four, rather than two.

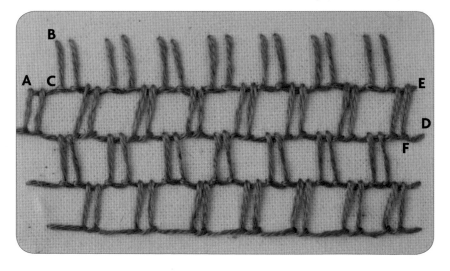

# Question 114:
# How do I work cloud filling stitch?

This stitch makes an attractive, open filling that can be used to add texture to large- and medium-sized areas reasonably quickly.

If you want to create this stitch very neatly, mark your fabric with parallel horizontal lines before you begin

## HOW IT'S DONE

**1** Work a row of small, evenly spaced straight stitches vertically across the first marked line.

**2** On the line beneath, work a second row of these stitches in the gaps between, rather than directly beneath each of the first stitches.

**3** Continue to produce these alternating rows until the area has been filled. Then, using a blunt needle threaded with a toning or contrasting colour, bring the needle up through the fabric from the wrong side towards the right at Point A.

**4** Pass the needle through the first stitch on the top row, and then take it through the first stitch on the row below.

**5** Continue lacing though the stitches until you reach the end of this first row.

**6** Reinsert the needle at Point B. To begin the next row, bring the needle up again at Point C and lace along towards the right, reinserting it at the end of the row at Point D. Continue to work rows in the same way until the shape has been filled.

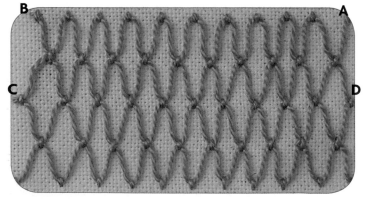

*LEFT* Cloud filling stitch is easy to work evenly if marked out before you begin stitching.

# Question 115:
# How do I fill a space with satin stitch?

For most accurate results, first mark out on your fabric the shape to be filled. Then, working from left to right, bring the needle up through the fabric from the wrong side to the right at Point A. Reinsert the needle at Point B. Bring it up again at Point C, down again at Point D and up again at Point E. Repeat as necessary until the shape is completely filled. There should be no ground fabric visible between the stitches.

*TOP LEFT* To fill an area with satin stitch, mark out the shape.
*TOP RIGHT* To work a sloping satin stitch, start at the centre of the shape, and work towards the right.
*BOTTOM LEFT* Continue satin stitching to the right until half of the shape is filled.
*BOTTOM RIGHT* Return to the centre of the shape and continue satin stitching to the left until the shape is completely filled in.

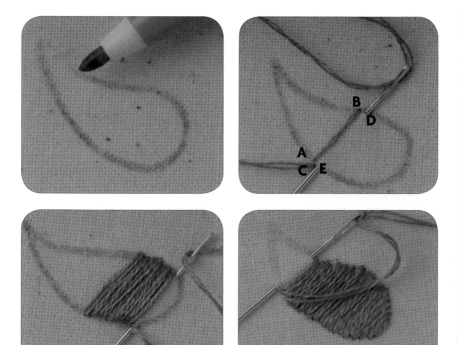

# Question 116:
# How do I fill a space with split stitch?

This stitch is best worked with a soft, untwisted thread. When you are experienced in this stitch, you may like to try working it with a needle threaded with two colours, splitting the stitch between the two colours each time.

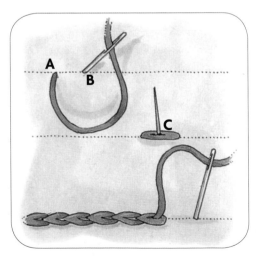

*LEFT* Split stitch is a quick and satisfying filling stitch to work.

# Question 117:
## What is padded satin stitching?

Padded satin stitching is a solid, smooth filling especially suitable for giving an embossed, three-dimensional look to small areas. Worked in a thread with a sheen, such as stranded embroidery cotton, it produces a lustrous, elegant finish. Padded satin stitch is most successful when worked on smooth or finely woven fabric. It consists of a top layer of satin stitches, worked in an opposing direction to the supporting layer of stitching beneath. This top layer of stitches is often worked at a slanted angle.

The hallmarks of a well worked classic padded satin stitch are that the edge of the shape should be cleanly defined and smooth, rather than jagged, and that the satin stitches themselves are perfectly parallel to each other with no space or padding stitch visible beneath them.

*BELOW* Satin stitch gives your work a three-dimensional look.

# Question 118:
# How do I use padded satin stitching as a filling stitch?

Mark out the shape to be filled on your fabric and work around the outline of your shape in split stitch. Then decide in which direction you want the uppermost layer of stitches to slant. Working your stitches at a right angle to that of your final layer, use satin stitch to fill the area, stitching just over the split stitch outline. Finally, work the top layer of satin stitch over this base at right angles to the padding stitches. Use the same thread for all stitches to achieve a smooth, polished result.

As with all types of freeform embroidery though, rules are there to be broken, and there is no reason why you should not experiment with breaking this stitch down and mutating it into a different form; for example by working the base stitch in a different colour, and deliberately leaving occasional gaps between the parallel top stitches. In experimenting with traditional stitches, you will find that there is a point at which if you do not respect at least one element of the classic instructions for working it – for example in satin stitch, if the stitches are not parallel to each other – the stitch loses its defining characteristics and becomes something else entirely. This might or might not be a visual success. Only you, the fearless freeform embroiderer, can decide!

## EXPERT TIP
**❝ For a very raised look, work padded satin stitch over felt or card. ❞**

# Question 119:
# How do I work basketweave stitch?

# Question 120:
# When is Jacobean couching used?

Jacobean couching is useful for filling large areas as it covers a lot of ground relatively quickly.

# Question 121:
# How do I work Jacobean couching?

Bring the needle up through the fabric from the wrong side to the right at Point A and pull through. Reinsert the needle at Point B.

Continue making long, parallel straight stitches across the shape to be filled. Then lay more parallel threads at a 45-degree angle across the first row of threads, forming a diamond grid.

Finally, using a contrasting thread, make a long straight stitch at each intersection, from Point a to Point b on each one, followed by a small securing stitch from Point c to d, holding all the threads in place.

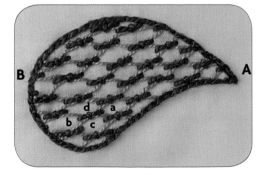

*RIGHT* Jacobean couching is a complex looking, but easy to work, filling stitch.

# Question 122:
## What is flat stitch?

Flat stitch is a generic term used to describe a group of stitches that have a flat overall appearance, even if they may actually be interlaced in their construction. In flat stitch, individual stitches are made without looping or crossing the thread. These stitches are widely used to create broken or unbroken lines, fill shapes and create geometric designs.

Running stitch, (see page 48, question 43), satin stitch, (see page 66, question 58) and fishbone stitch (see page 125 question 111) are all generally classed as straight or flat stitches. Backstitch (see page 50, question 46) is also sometimes included in this category.

*BELOW* Despite its name, flat stitch actually gives a richly dimensional look.

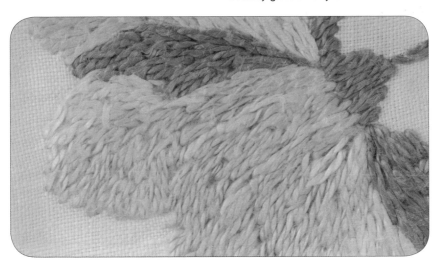

# Question 123:
## When is flat stitch used?

Flat stitches are generally used either as outlining or filling stitches.

# Question 124:
# How do I choose which flat stitch to use?

Choose a stitch to enhance the mood of your piece. For example, satin stitch produces a smooth, elegant look perfect for filling in organic leaf and petal shapes, whereas basketweave stitch is geometric and orderly, and is better suited to filling or suggesting buildings or other inorganic structures.

*BELOW* Satin stitch and shaded satin stitch add texture to essentially flat stitches when worked in carefully chosen colours.

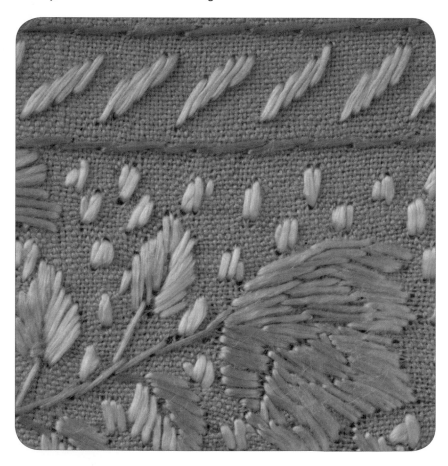

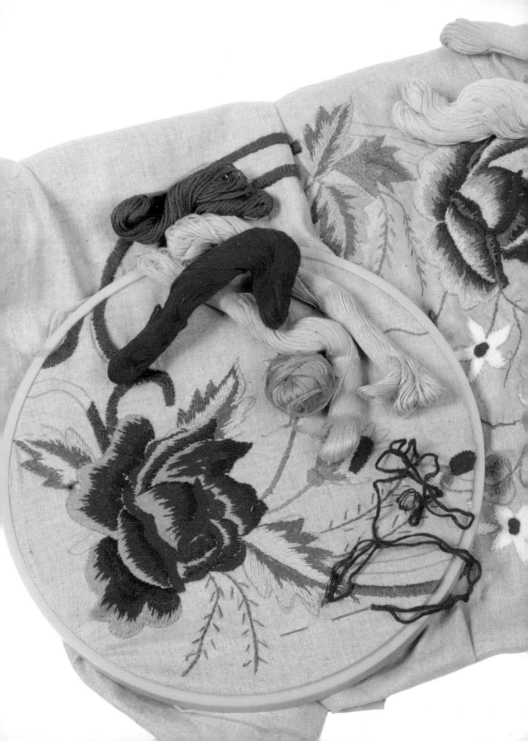

# 11
# DECORATIVE DETACHED AND LINKED STITCHES

These charming, quick-to-work stitches are often used to represent flowers and foliage. The same stitch may be worked at any scale and in a variety of threads to great dramatic effect.

# Question 125:
## How do I work twisted straight stitch?

### HOW IT'S DONE

This stitch, also known as twisted satin stitch, can be worked individually or close together in groups.

**1** Bring the needle up through the fabric from the wrong side to the right at Point A.

**2** Reinsert the needle at Point B, bring it out again at Point A, and pull the thread through.

**3** Slide the needle beneath the stitch and gently pull through. Then insert the needle very slightly above Point B and come out again at Point A again, ready to begin the next stitch or place the next stitch as desired.

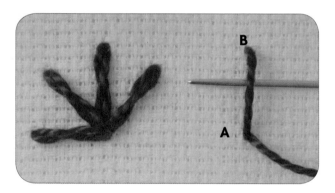

*ABOVE* Taking the thread below the first part of a twisted straight stitch.

*RIGHT* Wrapping the thread around before reinserting it to complete the second part of the twisted straight stitch.

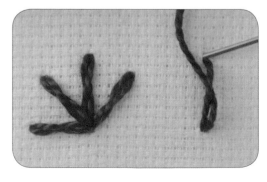

**Decorative Detached and Linked Stitches**

# Question 126:
# When is padded straight stitch used?

Padded straight stitch, also known as padded satin stitch, is used anywhere an extra-dimensional quality is required, but especially to fill small areas and illustrate natural, curvilinear forms such as leaves, flowers and berries.

## EXPERT TIP

**66** Work padded straight stitch over rows of chain, stem, or running stitch as you prefer, or, for a very raised effect, felt or card. **99**

*BELOW* A padded satin stitch bee worked by the author, with appliqué lace wings and flowers.

**Decorative Detached and Linked Stitches**

# Question 127:
## What is double knot stitch?

Double knot stitch is a delicately knotted stitch also known as Smyrna stitch, Palestrina stitch, tied knot stitch and Old English stitch.

# Question 128:
## When is double knot stitch used?

This versatile stitch can be used singly, for example as a small floral motif, or linked to form daintily knotted curved and straight borders and lines.

*BELOW* Double knot stitch produces a delicate, but textural line.

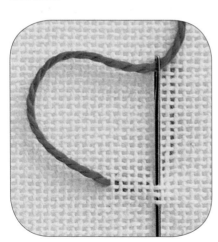

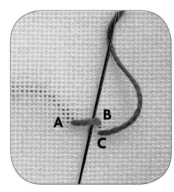

**Decorative Detached and Linked Stitches**

# Question 129:
# How do I work double knot stitch?

## HOW IT'S DONE

**1** Working from left to right, bring the needle up through the fabric from the wrong side to the right at Point A.

**2** Reinsert the needle at Point B and bring it up again at Point C, making a small stitch across the stitching line.

**3** Pass the needle from the top to the bottom of the previous stitch without piercing the fabric and gently pull through, leaving a small loop.

**4** Using your left thumb, hold this loop in place down and towards the left.

**5** Pass the needle through the same stitch again, working from top to bottom without piercing the fabric, as before and directing the needle to the right of the loop.

**6** Keep the thread held under the needle tip before, and pulling the thread gently to tighten. Repeat the stitch singly, with even spaces between, or adjoining each other as required.

# Question 130:
# When is detached chain stitch used?

Detached chain stitch can be arranged in a regular pattern, for example to suggest a natural texture in a landscape, sprinkled randomly to represent foliage, or placed in a gently graduating pattern to suggest shading and distance.

## EXPERT TIP
66 Detached chain stitch worked with a longer stitch to hold down the loop depicts a flower bud on a stem beautifully. 99

*BELOW* Detached chain stitch worked to form flower petals.

**Decorative Detached and Linked Stitches**

# Question 131:
# How do I work detached chain stitch?

## HOW IT'S DONE

**1** Bring the needle up through the fabric from the wrong side to the right at Point A and then reinsert it at Point A, leaving a loop of thread on the surface.

**2** Bring the needle up again at Point B, inside the loop, holding the thread down beneath the needle tip.

**3** Reinsert the needle at Point C, immediately outside the loop, to secure it in place.

## EXPERT TIP

66 **When working this stitch, take care to keep the tension gentle, so that the loop remains open.** 99

*LEFT* Daisy-like flowers are easily worked in detached chain stitch.

# Question 132:
# How do I work detached chain stitch to make a flower?

Work six stitches in a circle, as if forming the spokes of a wheel, producing a daisy-like design.

Alternatively, work a single stitch to represent a flower bud.

Another option is to work the stitch with a longer tail extending from within the loop to suggest a flower or foliage bud and stem.

*BELOW* Detached chain stitch is quickly worked, here on a handpainted ground.

# Question 133:
# What is wheatear stitch?

Wheatear stitch, as its name suggests, is often used to represent the ears of wheat it resembles.

That said, the wheatear stitch is much more versatile than having its use restricted to representing its namesake. As a delicate, sprinkled stitch, it can resemble seeds in flight, such as those of the sycamore tree. Also, with the addition of a detached chain stitch (see page 146, question 130) beneath it, a rabbit motif may be quickly created. In this case, work the detached chain stitch so that its securing stitch is at the base of the motif, forming the rabbit's tail.

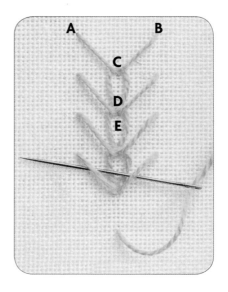

*ABOVE* Wheatear stitch can be worked simply or as a filling stitch.

# Question 134:
# How do I work wheatear stitch?

Wheatear stitch may be worked in any direction, scattered randomly or placed evenly to suggest, for example, a farm landscape.

## HOW IT'S DONE

**1** Bring the needle up through the fabric from the wrong side to the right at Point A and reinsert it at Point B.

**2** Pull through, leaving a loop of thread on the surface.

**3** Bring the needle up again at Point C, inside the loop. Gently pull through. Make a detached chain stitch and reinsert the needle at Point C, leaving a further loop of thread on the surface.

**4** Bring the needle up at Point D inside this second loop before reinserting the needle at Point E, just beyond the loop, to secure the detached chain stitch.

# Question 135:
# How and why would I link wheatear stitch?

Wheatear stitch can be stitched in a line worked from the top down, followed by a single, long, straight stitch, to represent stemmed ears of wheat as opposed to single grains. It can also be worked in parallel rows or in rows facing each other as an attractive border.

# Question 136:
## Is fern stitch a detached or linked stitch?

Fern stitch can be worked as either a detached or a linked stitch. As a detached stitch, it consists of three straight stitches radiating out from a single point at the base. The stitches may be of equal length, or varied, depending on what effect you require. To link the stitch, the groups of three stitches are worked in lines resembling branches or stems of foliage.

# Question 137:
## In what direction is linked fern stitch worked?

Work fern stitch from top to bottom, i.e. from the pointed tip of the fern shape down towards the base.

# Question 138:
## How do I work a line of fern stitch?

As its name suggests, fern stitch is ideally suited to depicting delicate, fern-like foliage. When worked in a line, this may be straight or curved to form a branch. Since fern stitch is basically a series of straight stitches radiating from the same hole, it is a really simple stitch to work.

Because fern stitch is so simple and obliging, lines of it may be worked on all kinds of fabric and using various thread types. You may prefer to draw out a line (see, transferring a design, see page 189, question 171) before starting to stitch or to stitch in a totally freestyle way, letting the line find its own direction as you stitch.

A simple but effective technique in freeform embroidery is to take a meandering line of stitch over and across various layers of fabric, joined either by patchwork (see picture on page 55, question 51 of lines of chain stitch worked across patchwork), or appliqué (see Chapter 14 on appliqué techniques).

## HOW IT'S DONE

**1** Working from the top of the line you wish to stitch, bring the needle up through the fabric from the back to the front at Point A.

**2** Reinsert the needle at Point B and bring it out again at Point C.

**3** Reinsert the needle at Point A and bring it out at Point D.

**4** Reinsert the needle at Point A and bring it out again at Point E.

**5** Reinsert the needle at Point F before bringing it out again at Point F and out at Point G. Continue this way until the line is the required length.

*RIGHT* Fern stitch is a simple but useful stitch, comprising of three straight stitches.

# Question 139:
# When is backstitch used as a detached stitch?

Backstitch can be used in a detached form where you wish an area to be filled, but retain an open, airy effect. Used in this way, it is also referred to as seed stitch or dot stitch.

To work it, simply place small backstitches randomly or in deliberate patterns across the area to be filled. Work the stitches singly or in pairs placed very closely side by side for added definition.

*BELOW* Even in a single colour, detached backstitch gives a lively, bold look.

# Question 140:
# What is star stitch?

Star stitch is a simply worked stitch of radiating lines, usually numbering between six and ten, resembling a star.

# Question 141:
# When is star stitch used?

Star stitch is an obvious choice for depicting stars in a night sky, but is also highly effective for representing simple, daisy-like flowers. As well as its use for depicting individual motifs, star stitch can be worked randomly scattered or evenly placed as a background or filling stitch.

# Question 142:
# How do I work star stitch?

A star stitch may be worked in any direction. For a regular, even result, mark a circle on your fabric, divided by lines according to your preference. Six, eight or ten points work well. Star stitches worked with too many points tend to develop lumpy centres.

Varying the number of points within a group of star stitches gives dynamism and variety to your piece.

## HOW IT'S DONE

**1** Bring the needle up through the fabric from the wrong side to the right side at Point A.

**2** Take it down again at Point B before bringing it up again at Point C.

**3** Reinsert the needle at Point B before bringing it up again at Point D and reinserting it at Point B.

**4** Continue your way around the circle, making sure that all stitches end in the centre.

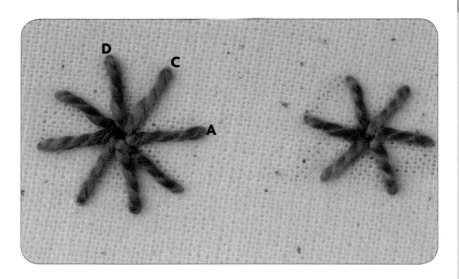

*ABOVE* Star stitch worked with varying numbers of stitches.

# Question 143:
# What is upright cross-stitch?

An upright cross-stitch is also known as the Saint George cross-stitch. It is exactly as its name suggests – a cross-stitch that is turned 45 degrees so that the arms are vertical and horizontal instead of diagonal.

> ## EXPERT TIP
> 66 **Upright cross-stitches work well for couching narrow ribbons, as these also provide guidance for the size of the crosses.** 99

## Question 144:
# When is upright cross-stitch used?

Upright cross-stitches can be worked individually, in lines, in a scattered, random pattern, or regularly and closely to produce a dense, even filling stitch. The latter arrangement is often used in blackwork.

## Question 145:
# How do I work upright cross-stitch?

If you are working on a group of individual upright cross-stitches, even if you are placing them in a random manner, their appearance will be improved if the top threads are worked in the same direction.

### HOW IT'S DONE

**1** Working from left to right, bring the needle up through the fabric from the wrong side to the right at Point A.

**2** Reinsert the needle at Point B. Continue in this way, spacing the stitches as you desire.

**3** Now travel back along the line of stitches, adding the vertical line of the cross by bringing the needle up through the fabric at Point C and down again at Point D.

*BELOW* Upright cross-stitch worked in varying scales.

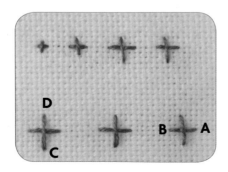

# Question 146:
## What is scroll stitch?

Scroll stitch is a textural, knotted stitch ideally suited to producing curvilinear designs with a flowing, naturalistic look. It is also used to make borders.

*BELOW* A working scroll stitch.

*LEFT* Scroll stitch is perfect for bordering marine- or aquatic-themed work.

# Question 147:
# How do I work scroll stitch?

## HOW IT'S DONE

For the most textural appearance, choose a robust, round thread to give maximum definition to the knots.

**1** Working from left to right, bring the needle up through the fabric from the wrong side to the right at Point A.

**2** Make a loop in the thread in a clockwise direction and hold this down with your left thumb.

**3** Reinsert the needle at Point B and bring it out again at Point C, keeping the loop of thread beneath the needle.

**4** Pull gently through. Repeat, spacing the scrolls as you wish.

**5** For a neat, even result, take care to ensure that all scrolls are the same size. Finish off the last scroll with a small securing stitch.

Scroll stitches look wonderful embellished with a spherical bead placed at the centre of each scroll (see Chapter 13, 'Attaching Sequins, Beads, Buttons and Charms'; question 159 and question 160 for general advice on beading). Have fun experimenting with the size of the scrolls and also the beads. You will be amazed at the different results you can achieve just by varying these elements. For example, work the scrolls quite small, and sit a bead at the centre of each one, almost like a cherry on a cupcake; or make the scrolls quite large, open and airy, and the centrally placed bead resembles the centre of a whirlpool.

Working rows of scroll stitch not only close to each other, but actually running over and across each other, produces a very rich, almost encrusted look. Keep to a single colour for a restrained, but still textural, appeal or use contrasting shades for a riotous scramble of colour and shape.

Scroll stitch also works well stitched into a spiral, producing floral-type shapes. Again, it is fun to embellish these with beads after you have worked the scroll stitch itself.

# Question 148:
## How do I work rope stitch?

### HOW IT'S DONE

Use a firm, rounded thread for best effect, and work this stitch from top to bottom.

**1** Bring the needle up through the fabric from the wrong side to the right at Point A and reinsert it at Point B.

**2** Form a loop with the thread around the front of the needle and then beneath the needle tip.

**3** Bring the needle up again at Point C, inside the loop.

**4** Gently pull the needle through. Make a loop with the thread and insert the needle at Point D, right into the heart of the last stitch, almost beneath the threads.

**5** Bring the needle up again at Point E, inside the loop.

**6** Carefully pull the thread towards you to tighten the stitch. Continue to work stitches in this way, securing the last loop with a small stitch.

*RIGHT* Rope stitch is a wonderfully dimensional outlining stitch.

**Decorative Detached and Linked Stitches**

# Question 149:
# How do I work Spanish knotted feather stitch?

## HOW IT'S DONE

**1** Bring the needle through from the back of the fabric to the front at Point A.

**2** Make a loop up and towards the left and hold down the thread towards the left with your left thumb before inserting the needle at Point B.

**3** Take a slanting stitch down to the left, through the fabric, holding down the loop of thread. Bring the needle out again at Point C.

**4** Pull the thread through with the needle point held over the looped, working thread.

**5** Reinsert the needle just to the left of Point A, at Point D.

**6** Bring the needle up at Point E, making a loop beneath the needle from left to right. Carefully pull through.

**7** Slide the needle beneath the lower part of the square created between the first two stitches, reinserting the needle at Point F.

**8** Bring the needle out again at Point G. Repeat the sequence until you have worked a stitched line of your desired length. Secure with a final, small stitch.

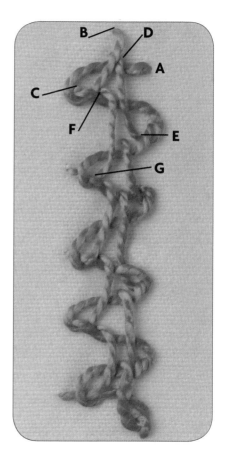

*ABOVE* Spanish knotted feather stitch is difficult, but satisfying to master.

# Question 150:
# How do I link Spanish knotted feather stitch?

Spanish knotted feather stitch may be worked in adjacent rows to produce a richly textured border or filling stitch. Keep the lines parallel for best effect by marking lines on your fabric before you begin.

This stitch produces sumptuous textured lines redolent of rich, knotted braid. There is no denying that achieving competency at this level of complexity takes plenty of time and patience.

Heavy, twisted threads such as coton perlé work particularly well. Adjacent rows of this stitch create stunning edgings for garments and home furnishings. Practise this stitch on spare fabric until you are totally comfortable with working it. When you are thoroughly familiar with the way the stitch develops, you will find that the work grows at a surprisingly fast pace.

The most critical thing to master when working this stitch is the tensioning as you pull the stitches to form and firm them. Take care not to pull the thread too tightly, as the fabric will easily pucker.

## EXPERT TIP

66 Along your way to producing a 'textbook' version of learning a new stitch, you may well discover hybrid stitches or ways of working it that yield interesting results, such as by changing the sizes of loops and knots. 99

# 12

# ADDITIONAL DECORATIVE STITCHES

This chapter includes unusual stitches that will add extra dimension to your work. Some require a degree of concentration to master, but will reward your initial effort in learning them.

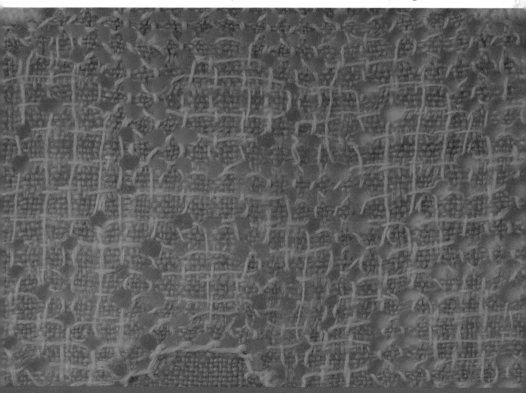

# Question 151:
# How do I make thread purl?

Thread purl is the contemporary equivalent of the metal purl with which seventeenth-century embroiderers embellished their raised work. This modern version is visually striking and fun to produce.

Wrap cotton or silk threads around a needle of the width that you want your finished purl to be. Wrap the threads tightly, close to the needle's point, but leaving a small space before the point. Then, wrap around a dozen times or more, depending on the type of effect you are seeking.

Use a small paintbrush to coat the threads carefully with PVA glue. Although this will be white when applied, it will dry clear. After about 30 seconds, ease the threads slightly closer to the needle's point in order to stop the threads sticking in situ.

When the glue has dried thoroughly, carefully ease the coiled thread off the needle and cut the purl to your chosen length. If you need a lot of purl for your project – e.g. for producing a foliage effect or depicting hair on a portrait – you will probably want to work on several needles at once to save time waiting for the glue to dry.

Arrange the needles loosely, like flowers, eye-side down in a small glass or similar vessel, so that the threads can dry evenly and without sticking to each other.

To affix the purl to your work, simply stitch it on as if it was a bugle bead, i.e. threading the needle up through your work, along the core of the purl and down through your work again, or use the method described for stitching on bugle beads so that they stand on end. Leave the ends of the purl long, or trim neatly, according to your design.

*OPPOSITE PAGE* Velvet stitch produces a deliciously tactile looped stitch that may be left as is or cut for a tufted look.

*LEFT* Thread purl is useful for depicting hair and is quick and fun to make.

# Question 152:
# How do I work velvet stitch?

## HOW IT'S DONE

Velvet stitch forms a freestanding loop that is secure and durable. It can be left looped or cut to form a lively textural contrast in your work.

**1** Work the stitch in rows from left to right, starting at the base of the area you wish to embroider. Bring the needle up through the fabric from the wrong side to the right at Point A and reinsert it at Point B.

**2** Bring the needle up again at Point A and form a loop before taking the needle back down again at Point B.

**3** Bring the needle up at Point C, keeping the needle below the loop.

**4** Reinsert the needle at Point D, making a cross-stitch.

**5** Bring the needle up again at Point C and pull through firmly.

**6** Repeat until you reach the end of the row, then fasten off the thread, leaving a long tail on the surface of the work if you are going to cut the loops.

**7** Work the next row from left to right. Bring the needle up through the fabric at Point D of the first stitch in the preceding row and work as before. If desired, cut loops after stitching.

# Question 153:
## What is insertion stitch?

An insertion stitch, also known as faggoting stitch, is a generic term used to describe stitches that create decorative, openwork seams between two pieces of fabric.

They were designed to join narrow widths of handwoven fabric in order to construct large items such as bedlinen, tablecloths and curtains.

# Question 154:
## How do I work insertion stitch?

If the pieces of fabric you are joining are not selvedged, and you require a neat rather than a raw finish to your piece, turn the edges of the fabric under and hem neatly.

## HOW IT'S DONE

**1** Cut a piece of sturdy, smooth paper approximately 7.5cm (3in) wide and the same length as the seam that is to be worked.

**2** Brown wrapping paper (kraft paper) is perfect for this purpose. Draw two parallel lines down the centre of the strip, spaced between 0.5cm (¼in) and 2.5cm (1in) apart as desired.

**3** Pin and tack the fabric edges to these marked lines.

**4** Using a thread suitable for the weight of your chosen fabric, work the insertion stitch of your choice to join the two pieces. Herringbone stitch is a popular and quickly worked choice.

## EXPERT TIP

66 Although any type of compatible thread may be used for insertion stitches, strong cotton thread is a reliable choice and a good thread with which to start this work. 99

# Question 155:
# What is a drawn thread stitch?

In drawn thread work, some of the ground fabric's threads are carefully pulled out of the weave, leaving the remaining threads available to be regrouped with a variety of decorative stitches.

This is a popular way of creating borders in conventional embroidery. In freeform work, you can use the technique innovatively, for example layering fabrics featuring drawn thread work to create depictions of fences, fields, pathways, etc.

*BELOW* Restrained when worked in a colour that matches the ground fabric, a simple drawn thread stitch adds discreet detail.

# Question 156:
## How do I prepare fabric for drawn thread work?

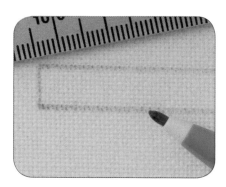

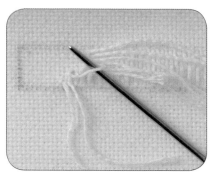

*ABOVE* To prepare an area for drawn thread work, first, mark out the space that is required.

*ABOVE* Cut through the horizontal threads at the centre of the marked area. With a blunt needle, draw out the threads, back to each side of the marked area. Make sure you have the number of threads desired to divide into the size of thread bundles required.

*RIGHT* Again, using a blunt needle, weave in the loose threads to secure each side of the marked-out area, taking the threads through towards the reverse of the fabric to begin.

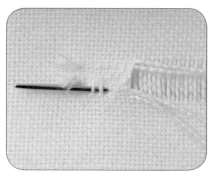

## HOW IT'S DONE

You will need an evenly woven ground fabric.

**1** To prepare the fabric, mark out the area to be worked.

**2** At the centre of the area, using small, sharp scissors, cut through the ground fabric's horizontal threads.

**3** Using a tapestry needle, carefully draw out the cut threads back to the sides of the marked area.

**4** Ensure that you have the correct number of vertical threads remaining for your chosen stitch.

**5** At each side edge of the cleared area, weave each thread back in towards the wrong side of the fabric for approximately 2.5cm (1in). Trim away excess thread.

## Question 157:
# How do I work a simple drawn thread stitch?

You will need an embroidery thread of similar weight to a single strand of the ground fabric thread and a tapestry needle. There are many types of drawn thread stitch. A simple way to get started is with hemstitch, also known as spoke stitch. This stitch secures the threads of a drawn thread border into groups, and can be used simultaneously to secure a hem, making it a useful stitch to master.

Make sure when preparing your fabric that you leave a number of vertical threads which is a multiple of your chosen thread groupings. Three to five is a good number with

which to start. Work from the wrong side of the fabric, from left to right. Fasten off your thread using the waste backstitch method. Bring the needle to the left of the first vertical thread, then up through the fabric and the top of the hem at Point A. Take the needle under four (or your desired number) vertical threads from right to left. Pull into a group. Take the needle to the right of the group and bring up again at Point B through the fabric and the top of the hem. Continue to the right. Secure and conceal the thread ends within the hem turning.

Having secured the thread to the left, take the needle to the left of your first vertical group of threads and up through the fabric at Point A.

Using a blunt needle, pass it from right to left across, then behind the group of threads, pulling them up into a bundle.

Take the needle down between this and the next group of threads and then up through the fabric again at Point B. Continue to the right.

## Question 158:
# How do I work around a corner in drawn thread stitch?

When stitching around a corner, work the groups of threads without a vertical stitch between them. These unadorned corners have a discreet elegance, but if you prefer, there are many stitches with which you can decorate them.

For example, for a buttonhole corner, work buttonhole stitch, with each stitch covering two threads of the ground fabric, along the corner's two outer edges. Catch the hem, if there is one, with these stitches and conceal the thread ends in the back of the buttonhole stitches.

To work a looped buttonhole corner, work buttonhole stitch along the two outer corners, two threads of your fabric deep. Leave yourself a long thread to make the loop.

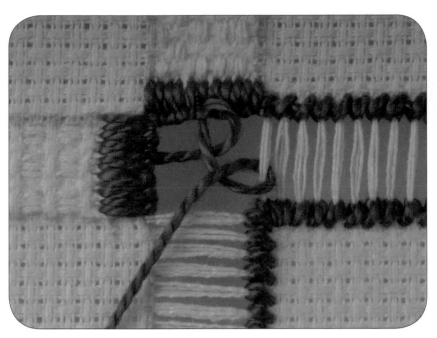

Run the long thread back through the buttonhole stitch, emerging at Point A. Take it over and back down through the buttonhole stitch at Point B. Take it over and around the first bundle of threads as shown.

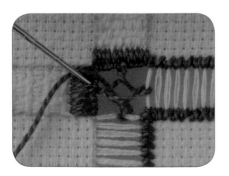

Take the thread over and around the next bundle of threads. Take it back over the buttonhole stitch where it first emerged, having passed under the stitch it formed there.

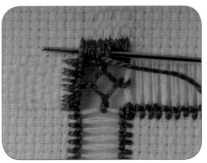

Ease the loop between your fingers until it achieves an even tension. Secure the loop by running the thread into the rear of the buttonhole stitch.

# 13

# ATTACHING SEQUINS, BEADS, BUTTONS AND CHARMS

Haberdashery, jewellery and craft suppliers carry a mouth-watering array of additional items to add sparkle and dimension to your work. These are simple to attach and create a wonderful contrast in texture to your freeform piece.

# Question 159:
# What needle do I use for beading?

The type of needle you choose will depend on what sort of bead you are using. Generally, fine, straight needles are used for beading. If you are adding only the occasional bead, any needle with an eye sufficiently fine to pass threaded through the bead will be acceptable. Sharps, betweens and quilting needles are all suitable if they are the right size for your bead. However, if you are sewing on a lot of fine, small beads, you will find it easier if you choose a beading needle. These very fine, straight needles have a long, thin eye and are flexible, making it easy for you to gather up several small beads at one time. Larger beads will generally be stitched on with thicker thread or yarn, so choose a larger needle accordingly, such as an embroidery, crewel, tapestry, or, for very large beads, a chenille needle.

# Question 160:
# What thread do I use for beading?

Specialist beading threads are available that make beading a much more pleasant experience than if you are using regular threads. This is especially the case when you are stitching on a lot of very small beads. Beading threads are strong, pliable and fine, and glide through the bead easily without fraying or looping. Cotton threads tend to fray, are difficult to thread through small beads, and knot and loop during stitching, as well as being prone to breaking. Beading threads can be waxed with colourless silicone wax, which greatly enhances their performance. Choose a thread colour that tones with your choice of beads and the background. Contrasting colours used with clear beads can also work well. For larger beads, have fun experimenting with the wide range of interesting yarns and threads available, such as metallics, nubbly textured handmade threads and even knitting yarn.

# Question 161:
# How and why do I use decorative stringing?

As well as stitching beads securely to the ground fabric in freeform embroidery, producing raised, dynamic textural areas on the surface of your piece, you can add beads that extend beyond the fabric itself.

This achieves an extra level of visual and tactile excitement and is very enjoyable to work. Use strung beads to extend the borders of your work by creating fringes or small areas of beaded fringe. For example, you could edge your finished piece with simple stitching or a twisted cord and embellish each corner with some strung beading. Strung beading is also very useful for drawing attention to details in a portrait, e.g. to depict jewellery or costume, or stamens in a floral picture. Following the guidelines for choosing beading

needles and thread, simply thread up your desired combination of beads so that they are suspended beyond the ground fabric. Use combinations of small beads to pull up into loops at the end of each string before taking the thread back up through the beads and into the ground fabric again. This end loop technique works best with an odd number of small beads, e.g. rocaille beads, and you will need at least five. The last bead strung before the smaller beads of the loop needs to be larger or of a different shape, for example a faceted bead or bugle bead.

## EXPERT TIP

**" Incorporating strung beads into your work is a satisfying way of giving new life to cherished, but unwearable jewellery, such as necklaces with broken clasps. "**

# Question 162:
# How do I attach a bugle bead?

Bugle beads may be attached either so that they lie flat or so that they stand up vertically from the fabric. The latter method, using rocaille beads in partnership with the bugle beads, is a useful way to represent flower stamens or other three-dimensional items.

To attach bugle beads so that they lie flat against the fabric, fasten on your thread, and bring the needle through from the wrong side to the right side, next to where you want to place the bead.

Thread the needle through the bead and reinsert it into the fabric at that end of the bead. Continue, fastening off with a few small stitches when you have finished.

To stitch on bugle beads so that they stand upright, fasten on your thread and bring the needle through from the wrong side to the right side at the point at which you want to place the bead.

Thread the needle through the bead, then through a small rocaille bead before taking the needle back through the bugle bead and down through the fabric again.

Continue as desired, securing your work with a few small stitches when you have finished.

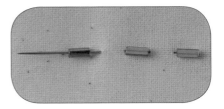

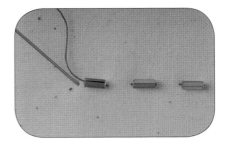

*RIGHT* Take the needle up through the fabric and through the bugle bead. Take the needle back through the fabric, placing it so that the bead sits neatly. Alternatively, add a rocaille bead after the bugle bead. Go back down through the bugle bead so that it stands away from the surface of the fabric.

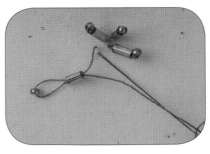

# Question 163:
# How do I attach a pendulous bead?

If you thread a pendulous bead directly on to your work, it will jut out at an ungainly angle. To hang droplet type beads attractively from your work, you will need to add some smaller beads alongside as described opposite.

## HOW IT'S DONE

**1** Make a small fastening stitch.

**2** Bring the needle up through the fabric from the wrong side to the right, in the position from which you wish the bead to hang.

**3** Thread the needle first through a small bead and then droplet bead.

**4** Add on the second bead before taking the needle back down through the fabric.

**5** Repeat as desired and finish off with a few small stitches.

*BELOW* Adding tiny beads beside a droplet bead helps it hang perfectly.

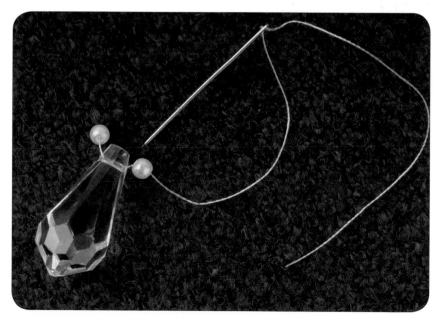

**Attaching Sequins, Beads, Buttons and Charms**

# Question 164:
# How do I attach a single sequin?

## HOW IT'S DONE

**1** Make a small fastening stitch.

**2** Bring the needle up through the fabric from the wrong side towards the right, passing through the centre of the sequin.

**3** Make a short horizontal stitch across the radius of the sequin, towards the right, before bringing the needle up through the fabric again just at the sequin's left-hand edge.

**4** Reinsert the needle through the sequin's hole.

**5** If you are attaching additional sequins in a row, bring the needle up through the fabric again to the left, ready to come up through the hole in the next sequin.

**6** Continue in the same way so that the sequins just touch, or place them individually as desired.

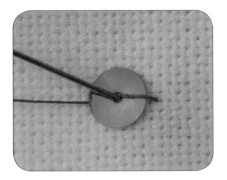

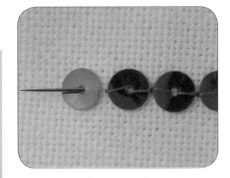

## EXPERT TIP

**❝ When stitching a row of overlapping sequins, flat sequins are easier to handle than faceted ones, which are ideally suited to cradling a rocaille bead and being affixed singly. ❞**

*ABOVE* A simple sequin takes just seconds to apply.

# Question 165:
# How do I attach a sequin with a bead?

## HOW IT'S DONE

**1** Make a small fastening stitch.

**2** Bring the needle up through the fabric from the wrong side towards the right, passing through the centre of the sequin.

**3** Thread on a small bead.

**4** Take the needle back down through the sequin and the fabric and pull through so that the bead sits neatly on top of the sequin. Repeat as required.

*BELOW* So simple but so effective: sequins affixed with beads.

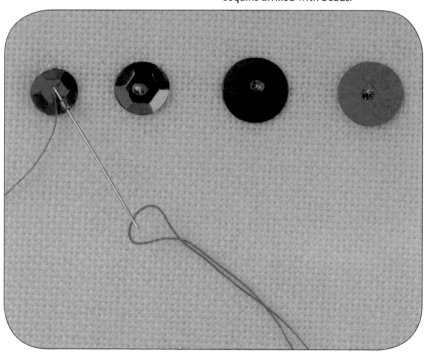

# Question 166:
# How do I stitch overlapping sequins?

## HOW IT'S DONE

**1** Make a small fastening stitch.

**2** Bring the needle up through the fabric from the wrong side towards the right, and up through the centre of the first sequin.

**3** Make a short horizontal straight stitch across the radius of the sequin, towards the right.

**4** Place the second sequin in position at the left-hand side, just overlapping the first one.

**5** Bring the needle up through the fabric and through the second sequin's hole.

**6** Make a straight stitch across to the right of this sequin, as before, going through the centre of the first sequin. Continue as required.

*BELOW* A row of overlapping sequins easily adds glamour to embroidery.

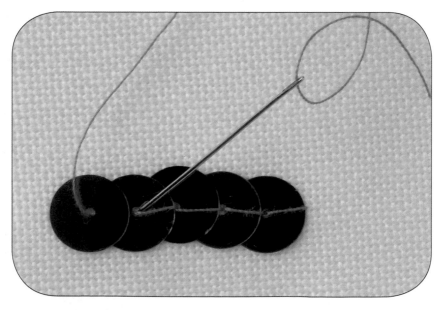

# Question 167:
# How do I attach a charm?

Charms have become increasingly popular as additions to freeform embroidery. Widely available in haberdashery departments and cardmaking supplies stores as well as from jewellers, they add personality and glamour to a piece.

## HOW IT'S DONE

**1** To stitch on a charm, use a strong thread and make sure you leave enough slack in the thread for the charm to sit on or dangle from your piece as required.

**2** Make several stitches, all evenly tensioned, and then contain and strengthen this group of threads by working buttonhole stitch around the length of bunched threads.

**3** Secure with small, neat, fastening stitches on the rear of your fabric.

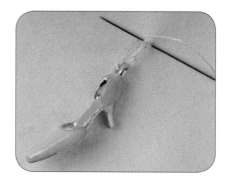

*FROM TOP TO BOTTOM*
1 Stitching on a charm adds impact with minimal effort.
2 Make several stitches to secure the charm.
3 Buttonhole stitch worked over the fixing threads is attractive and strengthening.

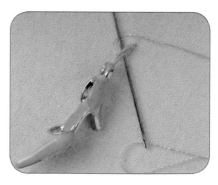

# Question 168:
# How and why do I attach buttons to my work?

Buttons add colour and dimension to a piece quickly and easily. They are ideal for depicting flower centres, wheels and trees or for kick-starting an abstract design. Buttons are most securely attached by using a doubled thread.

Four-holed buttons may be sewn on using either two sets of parallel stitches or crossed stitches. Buttons with shanks need just a few simple, securing stitches worked with a doubled thread for strength.

*BELOW* Buttons add a sleek contrasting texture to the softness of embroidery.

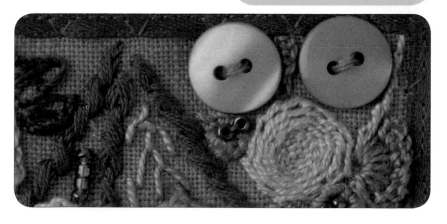

# 14

# APPLIQUÉ TECHNIQUES

Appliqué offers a quick and easy way of adding colour and texture to a ground fabric. There are several methods you can choose from depending on the look you are trying to create, so read about all of them before deciding.

# Question 169:
## What is appliqué?

Appliqué is the term used for the technique by which pieces of fabric are applied and secured on to a background. Sometimes the fabric pieces are embellished with decorative stitching that is also used to secure them to the background. Needleturn appliqué uses tiny, almost invisible stitching to secure the fabric to the background. Choose whichever method suits your design.

# Question 170:
## When is appliqué used?

Appliqué is a wonderful way of adding shape, pattern, colour and texture to a ground fabric quickly and simply. Designs can be as pictorial or abstract as you wish and can use almost any fabric. In fact, there is no need to limit yourself to materials strictly classed as fabrics. Plastic bags, handmade paper and scraps of glove leather are all suitable for appliqué, as well as the more traditionally used materials, such as felt and cotton.

*ABOVE* Start practising your appliqué technique using simple shapes.

# Question 171:
# How do I transfer a design for appliqué?

Place a piece of tracing paper over the shape to be transferred. Turn the tracing paper over and, using a soft pencil, scribble over the drawn outline. Turn the tracing paper back so it is right side up again. Place it on a clean sheet of paper or thin card and draw over the original outline once more to complete the transfer process. Draw over the transferred design if it is faint.

*FROM TOP TO BOTTOM*
1 Tracing over a shape with a soft pencil is a quick, easy way of transferring a design.

2 Scribbling over the reverse of the traced shape adds a layer of graphite ready for transferring your design.

3 You may need to go over faint lines with a pencil to strengthen them for additional clarity.

# Question 172:
## How do I cut and fold edges?

Snipping triangular notches into the seam allowance of curved shapes enables you to turn over their edges smoothly, retaining their flowing, organic form. In contrast, to produce crisp, angular points at the apex of a triangle, cut away the excess fabric from around the point.

At the inner angles of a zigzagged or triangular design, snip into the seam allowance almost right up to the marked line.

*RIGHT* Snip the edges of curved shapes before turning them for appliquéing to produce neat results.
*BELOW* Carefully fold over and tack your shapes prior to appliquéing them to the ground fabric to maintain accuracy and make the work easier to manage.

For all shapes, carefully fold over the seam allowance towards the wrong side of the motif, before pressing with a medium to hot iron and tacking down the edges to secure them temporarily before affixing to the ground fabric.

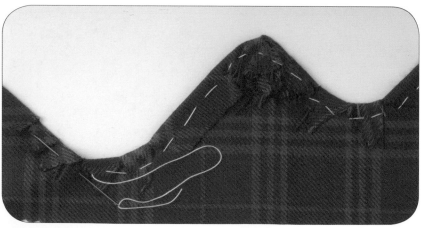

# Question 173:
# Why would I tack over a paper template?

Tacking over a paper template is an excellent, very controllable way of dealing with awkward shapes or where a high degree of accuracy is required in the look of the finished appliqué. It results in a neat, pre-turned fabric shape ready for applying to the ground fabric.

Cut out a paper template and draw around it on to a piece of fabric. Cut out the fabric, leaving a 5mm seam allowance all around the template.

Clip the fabric at tight curves and points to enable it to fold neatly over the paper, then place the template on the reverse of the fabric shape and ease the seam allowance evenly over the edges of the paper, securing with tacking stitches.

With a hot iron, press the reverse of the fabric and paper to define and secure the turned edge, then carefully remove the tacking stitches and discard the paper template. Pin the appliqué shape on to the background fabric and stitch in place using the stitch of your choice.

*BELOW* Tacking over a paper template ensures accuracy in appliqué.

# Question 174:
# How do I use fusible bonding web?

## HOW IT'S DONE

**1** Cut out a paper template in the desired shape of your appliqué motif.

**2** Lay the fusible bonding web on the wrong side of the fabric, paper side up.

**3** Cover with a pressing sheet and using an iron set to medium heat, press to activate the adhesive. Lay the template face down on the backing paper.

**4** Draw around the shape and cut it out. There is no need to leave a seam allowance since the bonding web will prevent the cut out shape from fraying.

**5** Remove the backing paper. Place the shape right side up on your background fabric and press to fix with a medium to hot iron. Embellish with stitches as desired.

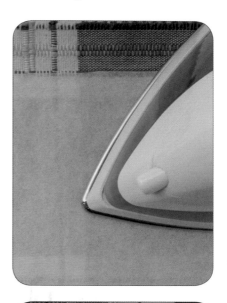

*TOP RIGHT* Ironing heat fusible web on to the reverse of fabric makes it, in effect, self-adhesive.
*BOTTOM RIGHT* Accurate, clean shapes can easily be cut from the non-fraying, web-backed fabric.

# Question 175:
## What is reverse appliqué?

In reverse appliqué, the design is cut out of the surface of the fabric to reveal an additional layer of fabric beneath. To work it, cut out a paper template of your chosen motif. Draw around the template on to your ground fabric. Draw another line 5mm (¼in) inside the shape. Cut out the shape, along this inside line. Using sharp scissors, clip the seam allowance to ensure smooth turning. Fold the seam allowance under and secure by pressing with a medium to hot iron. Pin a piece of contrasting

fabric into place behind your cut out shape. Stitch around the edge of the cut out shape to the fabric behind to secure in place and continue to decorate with stitches as required.

*RIGHT* Reverse appliqué adds an exciting depth to your background.

# Question 176:
## What stitches can I use to work appliqué?

Blanket stitch is a perennially popular edging stitch for appliqué, as it can be used to secure and decorate the applied fabric simultaneously. Feather stitch is another popular and attractive choice for the same reason. Other stitches that perform a similar dual function include running stitch, cross-stitch, stab stitch and French knots.

### EXPERT TIP
**66 When starting out in appliqué, keep the shapes simple, generously sized and bold for satisfying, encouraging results from the start. 99**

# 15

# 3D EMBROIDERY TECHNIQUES

This exciting group of stitches adds a thrillingly sculptural dimension to your work. You can produce very labour-intensive, detailed stitchery, or simply add found objects for a three-dimensional look for very little effort.

# Question 177:
## What is 3D embroidery?

3D embroidery is basically any embroidery that features raised surfaces. Although originally referred to as stumpwork, also known as raised embroidery (see page 198, question 180), 3D embroidery has come to mean stitching that stands proud on the surface. This can include found objects and non-traditional materials as well as padded stitchery. It is an innovative and very exciting area of embroidery.

# Question 178:
## What base fabrics should I use in 3D embroidery?

You will need to use a strong, evenly woven fabric that does not stretch, as it will have to take a lot of weight and changes in tension across the piece. Unwashed, unbleached, medium-weight calico is an excellent choice. It is neutral in colour, relatively inexpensive, sturdy, tightly woven and readily accepts colour in the form of paint or dye.

### EXPERT TIP

**66 If your finished piece is going to be in regular use, rather than being purely decorative, pre-wash your ground fabric before you start stitching, to reduce the risk of shrinking in future laundering. 99**

# Question 179:
# What decorative fabrics should I use in 3D embroidery?

In freeform embroidery, there are no hard and fast rules about the types of materials used, and nowhere is this more evident than in freeform 3D embroidery. Anything and everything can be used as a fabric including non-traditional materials such as pieces of coloured plastic bag, handmade paper and even thin metal, such as that used to manufacture drinks cans.

*BELOW* Organza, leather or even a fruit bag net are useful fabrics in freeform embroidery.

# Question 180:
# What is raised embroidery?

Traditionally, the term 'raised embroidery' refers to stump work. This type of embroidery, featuring stitching made three-dimensional by the addition of small, shaped wooden moulds and/or padding covered in stitching, was popular in the 17th century. Its appeal lasted well into the 19th century, and it has recently enjoyed a renaissance.

The term derives from embroidery 'on the stamp' or 'stump,' and is thought to refer to the wooden moulds or 'stumps,' or perhaps to have derived from the French word 'estompe,' meaning 'embossed'. Classical stumpwork is time consuming but rewarding. It features needlelace prominently. This is a fabric created entirely from embroidery stitches such as buttonhole stitch, which is worked separately and then applied to the ground fabric, over padded supports.

*BELOW* Raised embroidery fascinates viewers with its almost magically three-dimensional form.

# Question 181:
## How and why do I attach wire to my embroidery?

Wire is a very useful material for enhancing the three-dimensional aspects of freeform embroidery. Wire can be bent to any shape, and can be left bare for a contrasting texture, or may be bound, wrapped or stitched over as you wish. If you are binding wire with thread, do this before attaching the wire to the piece and leave a small amount of wire unwrapped at each end to be secured to the background fabric. Using a stiletto or similar tool, pierce a hole in the ground fabric just large enough for the wire to pass through. Insert the wire through the fabric, bend the end of the wire back towards the fabric, and secure firmly with stitching.

# Question 182:
## What is a slip?

A slip is a piece of embroidery worked separately from the main piece and then applied to it. This enables you to create incredibly rich, textural areas within your design. These slips can also be padded when they are applied to your ground fabric, adding a truly three-dimensional effect.

## EXPERT TIP

66 Slips are a great way of producing key areas of a piece without risking experimentation on your whole work. They are a particularly good way of applying faces, as these can be difficult to get right first time. 99

# Question 183:
## How do I make and apply a slip?

Work your slip in the design, colour and stitch of your choice. For example, to work a slip that is to be used as the upper part of a tree you might work green French knots closely over a green background slightly larger than the eventual size of the tree required.

### HOW IT'S DONE

**1** Cut out the shape, including a 5mm (¼in) seam allowance all the way around.

**2** Work running stitch around the perimeter, just inside the edge.

**3** Draw up the stitches so that the seam is turned under and adjust to the desired size and shape for application to the background.

**4** Pad the slip as required and stitch on to your background fabric.

# Question 184:
## What padding materials should I use in a slip?

An excellent choice for padding slips is loose polyester filling, sometimes called Dacron or Terylene, which will produce a padded effect without adding any unwelcome weight. Insert it behind the slip, a tiny amount at a time.

*RIGHT* The author adds synthetic wadding to an embroiderered muslin slip as she handstitches it to the satin ground of her piece.

# Question 185:
# How do I work a padded base?

## HOW IT'S DONE

**1** Draw the required shape on to the ground fabric.

**2** Draw off the shape to be filled and transfer it to a piece of felt.

**3** Cut the felt to precisely this size and shape and affix it inside the outline of the shape on the ground fabric, using small running stitches.

**4** As you stitch, gently ease the felt inwards, away from the drawn outline, to form sufficient space beneath the felt to hold soft filling.

**5** Leave a small gap in the stitching so you can add the filling until the felt has reached a sufficient depth of moulding for your design. Stitch the gap closed.

**6** Add further layers of fabric, independently worked needlelace, beading and embroidery until you are satisfied with the result.

# Question 186:
# How do I stitch over a padded base?

When you are applying needlelace or additional pieces of fabric to your padded base, use a toning thread and small, neat stitches.

Plan the work carefully so that the most important lines visually can be created by the rollover method. The piece to be added is stitched with its right side facing the right side of the ground fabric, so that when it is flipped back into place, the stitching is concealed and the smooth outline of the shape is maintained. Add decorative stitching and additional layers as required.

# Question 187:
# How do I stitch over a found object?

The incorporation of found objects into freeform embroidery is an exciting area of work. Practically any item can be utilised. Hardware stores are a particularly rich source of inspiration.

Washers, for example, can be stitched in place and covered simultaneously by buttonhole stitch. Tiny holes drilled into more unusual objects, such as twigs or other natural items, are easily made with an inexpensive hobby drill, enabling you to stitch these in place.

## EXPERT TIP

**❝ The list of materials suitable for stitching over is long and diverse. Everything from sections of plastic drinking straw to the blister packaging of pills can be given a new lease of life. ❞**

*BELOW* The author incorporating amber into a piece, using buttonhole stitch over a network of threads.

# 16
# DESIGN INSPIRATION

Inspiration is all around us. Very quickly, you will start to look at the world from a perspective of how you can translate what you see into stitch through freeform embroidery.

# Question 188:
# How do I begin to design my own work?

The starting point for your design can be anything that makes you want to pick up a needle and get stitching! Perhaps you have fallen in love with a spectacular hand-dyed thread and are itching to incorporate it into a piece, or have a cherished family photograph that is crying out to be translated into stitch. Sometimes the inspiration comes from the world around you. A walk in a bluebell wood sparks an idea of how those drifts of flowers, hazy in the twilight, would work well as massed French knots, possibly stitched on layered organza over a painted background to simulate a receding landscape. Ideas are everywhere, and once you become familiar with thinking about how concepts could be translated into stitch, you will increasingly see the world as one big inspiration for freeform embroidery!

*BELOW* Design ideas come from everywhere, the fabrics we use, the flowers we pick, the threads we love.

# Question 189:
# How do I plan my work?

It is a great discipline to note all your ideas down in a sketchbook, along with scraps of fabric, thread, pages torn from magazines, postcards and paint samples — in fact, anything that kick-starts the design process. As you collect and collate this information, your idea about a piece will gradually take shape. Some ideas will come almost ready formed. For example, if you want to translate a family photograph into embroidery and have already decided that you want to retain the photograph much as it is, the planning process will be pretty self-evident. You will need to make a note to obtain and prewash the ground fabric, and decide how you are going to get the image on to the cloth before stitching to enrich it. Conversely, a large, experimental, abstract piece inspired by an architectural detail photographed on holiday might require more thought. You might wish to diverge considerably from the original image, and to this end, some exploratory sketches and stitch samples would be a good idea before embarking on your finished piece. If you are going to texturise the background or use any experimental techniques, it is wise to try these out independently before applying them to your piece.

## EXPERT TIP

66 Don't get so concerned about producing a perfectly planned piece of work that you don't start it at all. It's better to simply get stitching than to prevaricate endlessly over an order of work. 99

# Question 190:
# How do I produce a stitch-themed piece?

Theming a piece around a particular stitch is a thoroughly enjoyable way of producing freeform embroidery because you can choose a stitch you really enjoy working. A piece developed from even a single stitch can be amazingly diverse. For example, if you particularly enjoy working straight stitch, an entire piece can be worked in this, yet look very varied if you use the stitch in a wide range of differing scales and weights of yarn and thread. Also try working the stitch over itself and over layers of fabric for a rich, textural appeal. Working on a ground pre-coloured with paint, ink, dye or photo transfer adds a surprisingly different dimension to the fabric with every single stitch, even if it is of the same type.

*BELOW* A single stitch, detached chain, inspired this breezy piece.

# Question 191:
# How do I produce a piece inspired by a photograph?

Photography is a great entry point to designing your own work. Inspiration is all around you. Your friends and family, architecture and the natural world are all terrific subjects. The advent of camera phones has meant that it has never been simpler to capture exciting images. Advances in technology have revolutionised textile art and now you can print photographic images directly on to fabric or on to specially treated paper, ready to transfer to fabric. (Copy shops can undertake this process for you if you prefer). The resulting image can then have embroidery added to highlight particular areas. For example, you might like to accentuate the eyelashes and hair on a portrait with textural stitching. Beads can also be used to great effect to focus the viewer's attention on key elements of a picture.

## EXPERT TIP

66 Working a version of a photograph in monotone can produce exciting results. There's no need to stick to black and white or sepia. Choose any colour you like and concentrate on variations in tone. 99

# Question 192:
# How do I use collage to design a piece?

Collage is the technique of sticking things on to a background and offers a very accessible starting point to designing your own work. It can be as immediate and speedy or as meticulous and painstaking as you wish. It requires no specialised draftsmanship skills and can be produced from almost anything you have on hand. Magazines, newspapers, giftwrap and other packaging materials are all good sources of colour, shape and texture. Simply tear or cut out shapes that appeal to you and assemble a design. Unless you have a particular plan in mind, working speedily and spontaneously will probably yield the most satisfying and enjoyable results. Trace off the resulting design or, if you have prefer, stitch directly on to the collage. If you don't want to stitch on to paper, you could transfer your collage on to fabric by scanning the collage into a computer and printing it on to iron-on transfer paper, then iron on to fabric.

*BELOW* A collage worked by the author kick starts an embroidery design.

# Question 193:
# How do I introduce texture to the background?

There is an ever-increasing array of options for adding a dimensional quality to backgrounds before stitching. Arts and craft suppliers carry a wide range of substances that can be applied to fabric and scraped, moulded and brushed into interesting textures that will remain stitchable. Gesso is a versatile choice for texturising, allowing you to create several distinct effects from a single product. This refined plaster is sold in liquid or powder form; the liquid form is particularly easy to use as it needs no preparation before application. Simply paint the liquid on to your fabric to create a distressed, soft surface that suits many types of freeform embroidery. Allow the gesso to dry thoroughly, after which it will readily accept colouring and embellishing with materials such as paint, ink, fabric-colouring wax crayons and metal leaf. Stitching into these finishes is immensely satisfying, and the results can be stunningly rich.

*BELOW* There are countless options for adding texture to backgrounds. Here, gesso, glitter, natural ores and powder paint have all been added randomly to a cotton fabric and left to dry.

# 17

# FINISHING

Paying as much attention to finishing your work as to the stitching of it is a very valuable habit to acquire. Consider your embroidery worthy of the best possible finishing techniques, and it will provide you with years of satisfaction.

# Question 194:
# What method of mounting should I choose?

To mount your work, you can use a flat board, such as acid-free mounting board or a stretcher frame. If you are going to frame your piece, choose a board or stretcher a little larger than the area you wish to display, as the frame edges will slightly encroach on your piece.

To mount your work on a board, lay the piece face down on a flat surface with the stretcher placed centrally on top. Using a staple gun or tacks and a hammer, fold and secure the edges of your piece up and over the stretcher. Secure in the centre of the top, then the centre of the bottom, and then in the centre of each side.

Then secure ether side of the centre top, then bottom, then at each side. Continue working on opposite edges alternately until you have worked your way around the entire frame. Fold in the corners neatly before securing. Your work is then ready to be framed or displayed as it is.

## EXPERT TIP

66 Mounting may not be the most thrilling aspect of freeform embroidery, but inadequate time and attention to detail spent at this time will make you slightly disappointed every time you look at your piece in the future, so only embark on this when you are feeling fresh and energetic. 99

# Question 195:
# How do I lace my work for mounting?

You can give your mount a softer look by first covering your board with a layer of wadding.

Simply wrap the wadding around the board and secure it to the rear with staples. Place your piece face down on a clean, flat surface and place the board centrally on top of the work. Fold over two opposing sides of the work and pin these in place, placing the pins in the side of the board.

As in stretcher mounting, begin centrally and work out, securing opposite sides alternately to keep the tension even (see question 194). When the whole piece has been pinned across two opposing sides, lace these sides together using strong, doubled thread.

As with the pinning process, begin lacing from the centre and work outward towards one side. Repeat on the other side, securing with a backstitch and leaving the thread ends long, then repeat the pinning and lacing process on the remaining two sides.

Fold in the corners. When the whole piece has been laced, you may find that you need to undo the securing backstitches and adjust the lacing to ensure an even tension across the whole piece before securing and trimming off the loose ends to finish.

*BELOW* It is well worth taking as much care with the lacing of your piece as you did with the embroidery itself.

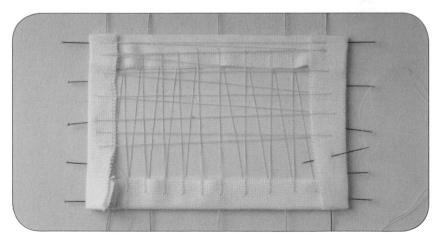

# Question 196:
# How do I press my work?

Most freeform embroidery pieces will become somewhat distorted during working and will need pressing to remove any creases that might have developed.

Place your piece face down on a well-padded surface such as a towel folded within cotton sheeting. The towel prevents the stitches from becoming flattened as they might on an ironing board, and the cotton fabric helps prevent the towel's loops from imprinting on the piece.

Preheat the iron depending on how much heat your ground fabric

*BELOW* Plan your hangings with generous borders to hide the sleeve and pole.

and threads can tolerate. If your work contains a mixture of materials, use a low heat. Cover your work with a piece of damp muslin and press the embroidered area lightly, using an up-and-down motion rather than ironing. Carefully press the background fabric and the work to dry.

## EXPERT TIP

66 **Take great care not to press areas of your work which incorporate sequins and other non-ironable materials.** 99

# Question 197:
# How do I hang work using the sleeve method?

Hanging work by the sleeve method is a popular choice for freeform embroidered pieces as it is simple to do, does not have the cost implications of framing, and, allows the texture of your work to be enjoyed unhindered by glazing.

Many sorts of pole can be used for hanging; choose one which suits your work. For example, a marine-inspired embroidery would sit happily beneath a piece of driftwood, while a geometric piece might be better suited to a sleek, stainless steel rod.

Cut the pole, rod or branch to a length approximately 10cm (4in) longer than the width of your work. From a suitable piece of fabric, cut a strip 5cm (2in) longer than the work is wide and with a depth sufficient to wrap comfortably around the pole, plus an additional 4.5cm (1¾in).

Turn under and hem each short end of the strip so that it measures the same width as your finished piece. Place the fabric strip along the top edge of the embroidery, right sides facing. Pin, tack, and machine stitch or hand-backstitch in place, 1.5cm (½in) from the edge of the strip.

Turn the strip right side out and press with a medium-to-hot iron, taking care to respect what type of fabrics you have used. If your fabrics are very delicate, press only with your hand.

Trial fit the pole before turning under the edge of the strip and then pinning, tacking and hand-slipstitching the strip in place, taking care that your stitches do not go through to the front of your piece. Reinsert the pole. You can suspend the work either by threading a cord through holes drilled at each end of the pole or by tying the cord firmly around each end.

Finish the ends of the cord as desired, for example with beads, tassels or decoratively tied knots.

## EXPERT TIP

**“ Non-traditional materials can make interesting visual punctuations to the ends of your sleeving cord, such as shells, pebbles and twigs. ”**

# Question 198:
# How do I make a twisted cord?

Although you can buy cord to edge, hang or decorate your work, it is easy and satisfying to produce your own; you can then make a cord of precisely the colour, texture and size you need to suit your piece. Almost any yarn or thread is suitable, including knitting yarns.

Cut two or more lengths, as desired, three times the finished length of cord required. Knot them together at one end and safety pin the knot to a fixed surface.

Standing sufficiently far away that the threads are taut, begin twisting the free ends in a single direction until the whole length is evenly and tightly twisted.

Placing your index finger at the centre of the twisted length, bring the knotted end and free end together. Remove your index finger and allow the threads to twist around each other to form the cord.

Knot the loose ends together and remove the pin. Even out the twists by running the cord carefully, but firmly, through your fingers. It is then ready to be used.

*BELOW* Twisted cord can easily be handmade to match the colours of your finished piece.

# Question 199:
## Should I frame my work, and if so, how?

You might prefer not to frame your work, as a major appeal of freeform embroidery is its rich, textural look and feel and even non-reflective glass hinders the immediacy of this appeal, but obviously your work will be kept cleaner and better preserved if it is framed, and this will affect your decision on whether to frame at all.

Work which is to be kept in a particularly textile-hostile atmosphere – e.g., a kitchen, where airborne grease and dirt will quickly accumulate – would be better preserved behind glass. If your work is very three-dimensional, choose a deep frame with a step or deep mount inside so that the stitching does not touch the glass. Ensure that the frame is completely sealed to prevent damage from condensation or pests.

### EXPERT TIP

**66 Non-reflective glass is more expensive than conventional glass, but a worthwhile investment for a significant piece of work. 99**

# Question 200:
# How do I care for my finished work?

Bright light, damp, dust and pests such as moths all have adverse effects on embroidery, so it is well worth bearing this in mind when displaying or storing your work. If you are storing a piece of work for any length of time, keep the work flat, protected by several layers of acid-free, conservation-grade tissue paper. If your piece is too large to be stored flat, you can roll it carefully around a cardboard tube that has been covered with the same type of tissue paper. The tube should be a minimum of 10cm (4in) in diameter, as a smaller tube could cause distortion of your stitches and the background fabric. Roll the work with its right side facing outwards as again this helps minimize the risk of distortion. Storing your

piece accompanied by your choice of sanded cedarwood blocks, proprietary moth deterrent products or lavender sachets will help deter these most destructive pests. To clean your work, unless you have made a piece designed so that it can be washed regularly, you will need to vacuum it at intervals using the following method. Cover your work with a piece of net curtain, secured all around the piece with pins, then vacuum the piece carefully, holding the nozzle at a little distance from the net.

*BELOW* What you will need for rolling a piece of embroidery prior to storage. Rolling the embroidery in tissue paper on a tissue covered card or plastic core helps keeps your work in optimum condition.

# Useful Information

## Thread and Yarn Demystifier

### Stranded embroidery thread

This glossy thread is inexpensive and widely available, making it a popular choice for embroiderers. Additionally, it is produced in an incredible array of colours, including variegated shades, and can be split into threads which may be used individually or in groups, for stitching of delicate or pronounced definition, as you prefer.

### Coton Perlé

This soft, single, twisted thread is perfect for creating boldly defined freeform embroidery. You do not need to split this thread before using. Round in cross section, its sharply defined twist holds the shape of a stitch well, and is a particularly good choice for braided and chain type stitches, which will look stunningly sculptural worked in coton perlé. It is available in random-dyed as well as plain shades, and in various thicknesses; the higher the number, the finer the thread.

### Coton à Broder

This is a highly twisted, single, fine and shiny thread.

### Soft Embroidery Cotton

This is a matt, fairly thick, loosely twisted single thread.

### Crewel Wool

This is a very fine, firmly twisted, strong 2-ply wool, available in a wide variety of subtle shades.

### Filo Floss

This is a soft, six-stranded plied silk with a rich sheen and a loose twist. It may be divided into one or more strands for finer work.

## Demystifying Metallic Threads

### Japanese Gold

This is 18ct real gold thread. As you might expect, it is expensive and not widely available.

### Imitation Japanese Gold

This, as its name suggests, is an imitation of the 18ct version. It is less expensive and is a very good substitute.

### Admiralty

This range of metallic threads has a percentage of real gold, but is not as expensive as Japanese 18ct gold thread.

### Gilt

This metallic thread is the least expensive option. It looks similar to the Admiralty thread initially, but it tarnishes more quickly.

# Web sites

## www.embroiderersguild.org.uk

With over 25,000 members, The Embroiderers' Guild is the UK's leading crafts association and educational charity, offering a comprehensive programme of contemporary exhibitions, workshops, courses, lectures and tours both in the UK and internationally.

No particular skill level is required for entry, and at any meeting, you will find interesting speakers and friendly stitchers keen to pass on their knowledge to new members. The breadth of techniques covered makes membership a highly cost-effective, and time-efficient investment for anyone with even a passing interest in embroidery. Highly recommended.

## www.twistedthread.com

If you only visit one show internationally a year, this is the website for your must-buy tickets. The Knitting and Stitching Show is the definitive exhibition for anyone passionate about cutting edge and traditional textiles alike. The name is slightly deceptive, as the scope of this show is jaw droppingly diverse in its scope.

Naturally, knitting and stitching are exceptionally well represented at all levels, but here you will also find a mouthwatering array of information and inspiration on techniques and materials to incorporate in your work. From felt-making to beading, mixed media to appliqué; this really is a one-stop shop for freeform embroiderers.

Manageable in one day, this show is ideal for a two day treat. This way, you can make the most of the workshops on offer, and have time to mull over all the inspiration you pick up on day one from the galleries and hundreds of specialist traders, ready to make planned purchases on day two. Sister show The Festival of Quilts is also well worth a trip, as it encompasses a wealth of surface decoration techniques such as transfer printing and hand painting as well as freeform embroidery itself.

## www.handembroidery.com

Hand and Lock has provided specialist and custom embroidery, monogramming and beading work for more than 200 years, yet marries this venerable tradition with a laudable ongoing commitment to developing current and cutting edge talent in embroidery. Its annual prize promotes the use of hand embroidered surface embellishment within the fashion, costume and interiors industries. Inspiring studio tours and classes are highly recommended. The online showcase of embroidery techniques encompasses the best contemporary design and fresh approaches to freeform embroidery, always to the highest possible standards. A must-visit website.

# Index